M000237067

Japanese Washi
PAPER CRAFTS

Seventeen Delightful Projects to Make
With Washi Paper

Robertta A. Uhl

TUTTLE PUBLISHING
Tokyo • Rutland, Vermont • Singapore

First published in 2002 by Tuttle Publishing,
an imprint of Periplus Editions (HK) Ltd.,
with editorial offices at 364 Innovation Drive,
North Clarendon, VT 05759

Copyright © 2002 Periplus Editions (HK) Ltd.

All rights reserved. No part of this publication may be
reproduced, stored in a retrieval system, or transmitted,
in any form or by any means, electronic, mechanical,
photocopying, recording or otherwise, without the prior
written permission of Tuttle Publishing.

ISBN-13: 978-0-8048-3813-9
ISBN-10: 0-8048-3813-5
LCC Card Number 2002108052

Previously published in 2002 as *Wonderful Ways with Washi*
ISBN: 0-8048-3344-3

Distributed by:

Japan
Tuttle Publishing
Yaekari Building, 3rd Floor
5-4-12 Osaki, Shinagawa-ku
Tokyo 141-0032
Tel (03) 5437 0171 Fax (03) 5437 0755
tuttle-sales@gol.com

North America, Latin America and Europe
Tuttle Publishing
364 Innovation Drive
North Clarendon, VT 05759-9436
Tel (802) 773 8930 Fax (802) 773 6993
info@tuttlepublishing.com
www.tuttlepublishing.com

Asia Pacific
Berkeley Books Pte Ltd
130 Joo Seng Road
#06-01 Olivine Building
Singapore 368357
Tel (65) 6280 1330 Fax (65) 6280 6290
inquiries@periplus.com.sg
www.periplus..com

Second edition
10 09 08 07 06
10 9 8 7 6 5 4 3 2 1

Printed in Singapore

TUTTLE PUBLISHING® is a registered trademark of Tuttle Publishing,
a division of Periplus Editions (HK) Ltd.

Contents

4

Introduction

Washi, literally "traditional Japanese paper", is the Japanese word for all types of paper, including traditional handmade sheets as well as similar-looking papers produced by modern manufacturing methods. This book, however, is concerned with the paper made by hand by artisans all over Japan.

Washi paper is the material of the craftsman, the painter, the calligrapher, the designer, the architect, and the tea master. Paper screens are an integral part of every house. People in both town and country use Japanese paper in all aspects of their daily lives: in umbrellas, fans, lanterns, lamps, containers, toys, origami, and other crafts. In Shinto rites, paper symbolizes the purifying aspect of the god.

Although the art of making paper was first developed in China, it spread to Japan in the seventh century AD along with Buddhism. Buddhist monks initially produced it for writing scriptures, but the flowering of a court culture during the Heian period (794–1192) created a demand for official papers and for decorated sheets for poetry and diaries. This, in turn, stimulated the development of government mills as well as a local cottage industry. The decline of the imperial court and the rise of the samurai warrior class after AD 1192, led to a demand for good-quality utility paper, while the development of printing and the architectural use of paper in sliding screens and doors added a new dimension to paper consumption. By the late 1800s, more than 100,000 Japanese families were making paper by hand for everyday use – for utensils, housing, and even clothing. After the opening of Japan to the West during the Meiji Restoration, mechanized paper-making technology was introduced to Japan, creating stiff competition for local paper-making households. However, a vigorous folk craft market from the mid-1920s, as well as a publishing boom after World War II, stimulated a demand for large quantities of handmade paper. Although only 350 families were still actively producing Washi in the mid-1990s, the unbelievable range of color, textures, and designs of the papers which continue to be produced, is testimony to Japan's unrivalled skill in all types of paper making. Japan continues to produce a greater quantity and variety and a higher quality of handmade paper than the rest of the world combined.

Washi is traditionally made by hand from the long inner fibers of the bark of three native plants: the kozo, mitsumata, and gampi. Kozo (*Broussonetia kazinoki*) is a shrub of the mulberry family. Reaching 3 meters at full growth, the plant is easy to cultivate and regenerates annually. The inner bast fiber is the longest, thickest and strongest of the three plants and is therefore the most widely used in paper-making; kozo is also considered the masculine element, the protector. Mitsumata (*Edgeworthia chrysantha*), a shrub of the daphne family, reaches a height of 2 meters. Graceful, delicate and soft – it is said to be the feminine element – it can be harvested only once every three years after planting and its paper is therefore more expensive. Because its fiber is thin and soft, it produces smooth paper with excellent printability. It is also insect resistant. Gampi (*Wikstroemia sikokiana*), like mitsumata, is a shrub of the daphne family, reaching a height of 2 meters when mature. The earliest fiber to be used for paper making, and considered to be the noblest because of its richness, dignity and longevity, the long, thin fibers produce the most lustrous of the three papers. However, the relative scarcity of the plant make its papers the most expensive. Other natural fibers, such as abaca, hemp, horsehair and rayon, as well as silver and gold foil, are sometimes used for making Washi or are mixed in with the other fibers for decorative effect.

The leaves and roots of a mulberry plant.

Pulverized mulberry roots being pressed into sheets in a boxed frame.

Sheets of paper put out to dry on boards before designs are stenciled on them.

To make Washi from the kozo mulberry, the plant is cut down to the root when mature, then cut in two. The top half is debarked and used as firewood. The bottom half is also debarked, then boiled until it turns black, and hung out to dry. The branches are then rinsed and stomped on by foot until they are soft and the fibers separate to form a pulp. The rough edges are stripped off before the fibers are once again rinsed and hung out to dry. They are then boiled again, this time with the ashes from the top part of the plant that was previously used as firewood. This mixture is then pulverized and a paste from the root of a plant called *taroimo*, which comes from the potato family, is added to the mixture. The wet mixture is then stacked together and gently pressed on to a boxed frame into sheets, causing the bark to become fibrous and interwoven. After the mixture has settled, the sheets are carefully separated and pulled out of the press, one at a time. Each sheet is brushed on to a framed board and set outside to dry. When the sheets are completely dry, they are ready to have the printed design stenciled on, a process similar to silk screening. One color is applied at a time until the desired design is completed. The finished Washi is then called Yuzen ("hand-printed patterned paper").

Since the long plant fibers that compose the paper are of uniform length (about 1/4") and become thoroughly intertwined during the paper-making process, Washi is very tough, flexible and durable; it does not tear like regular paper when dampened with paste and is said to last up to 1,000 years! Yet, it has a very soft texture and appearance, and because of its non-acidic components is extremely light. The thickness of Washi varies from lacy tissue to card stock. Its texture may be smooth, rough or crinkled. Because of the paper's natural qualities, it is not surprising that Washi is the favorite and most commonly used craft paper among the Japanese.

More recently, Westerners have begun to explore the possibilities of using this beautiful paper in their crafts. They are attracted to the colors, textures and weights of the paper, and also to the delightful designs, many of which capture the spirit of Japan's great textile tradition. Washi patterns range from classic motifs depicting Japan's rich cultural heritage (kimonos, fans, Kabuki actors) to motifs inspired by nature (bamboo, flowers, cranes). Not only are the motifs noteworthy for their elegance, delicacy, refinement, rich colors and attention to detail, but they are also executed with a wonderful sense of the abstract.

Westerners, like myself, who live in Japan, have discovered many enjoyable ways to use printed Washi. In this book, *Japanese Washi Paper Crafts*, I have included some of the most popular Washi projects that I teach. They are all elegant, creative, simple yet challenging, and the finished products are strikingly beautiful in any setting. These simple-to-make, hand-crafted projects, suitable for all occasions are presented in a series of easy-to-follow, step-by-step instructions. Each step is illustrated, for additional guidance. It is my hope that this book will help you to discover the wonderful Washi crafts that offer a delightful alternative to store-bought gifts — a wonderful way to leave a warm and lasting impression.

Shopping for Washi

Sizes: The standard size of a full sheet of printed Washi is 26" x 39". Some companies make smaller sized sheets, so it is wise to measure the sheets before buying. Some stores sell their printed Washi rolled up in plastic packaging with the size marked on the plastic cover. In Japan, the larger craft stores display their Washi flat in drawers or loosely folded and placed on specially designed wooden shelves.

One-way patterns: Some printed Washi papers have definite one-way patterns. You will need to take this into account when doing certain projects, such as covering milk cartons with Washi for the Oriental Vase and Cherry Blossom Box shown in this book. It is wise to buy a little extra printed Washi to ensure that the pattern is able to go in the same direction all around the container.

Economizing: When purchasing printed Washi, it is more economical to purchase full sheets than smaller pieces. If you want to have a variety of printed patterns at your disposal, a good way is to join with a group of friends in purchasing a large number of full sheets of printed Washi which you can then divide up among you, sharing the expense.

Borders: Full sheets of printed Washi have a solid, unprinted border around the outer edges. These edges should not be discarded but kept for covering the holes on the eggs when making Washi Covered Eggs.

Internet sites: Washi has become very popular in recent years and there are a large number of Washi sites on the Internet. These allow viewers to purchase Washi paper of all kinds, as well as instruction kits and books. Some of the more popular sites are www.washiart.com / www.kura.com / www.shizu.com / www.heian.com / www.kimscrane.com / www.ichiyoart.com / www.aitoh.com. A forthcoming site is www.washiways.com. This will carry my *Japanese Washi Paper Crafts* books, kits, and supplies.

A selection of hand-printed Washi.

Kokeshi Doll

This is a great craft idea for doll collectors. It also makes an ideal birthday gift for a little girl! Different sized cardboard tubes can be used to make dolls of various sizes. The hair of the dolls can be decorated in a number of ways – with ribbons, beads, artificial flowers and flower stamens.

EQUIPMENT AND MATERIALS

- 1 empty paper towel cardboard tube
- 2 empty toilet paper cardboard tubes
- 1 cardboard square (2 1/2" x 2 1/2")
- 1 solid (extruded) styrofoam (1 1/2") ball (not the air bubble kind)
- 1 rectangle of printed Washi (8 3/4" x 6") for the kimono
- 1 square of solid Washi (2 1/2" x 2 1/2")
- 2 rectangles of solid Washi (6" x 1 1/2") for around the neck and base
- 1 rectangle of crimped printed Washi (6" x 1 3/4")
- 1 rectangle of solid Washi (6" x 2")
- 1 rectangle of black crimped solid Washi (7" x 4") for the hair
- 1 rectangle of black crimped solid Washi (5" x 1 1/2") for the fringe/bangs
- 2 gold or silver cords (8" x 1/16")
- 1 gold or silver cord (7" x 1/8")
- 1 rectangle of gold Washi (1 1/2" x 1")
- 1 small straight pin
- Fine-tipped red and black felt tip markers
- Transparent (Scotch) tape
- Small sharp scissors
- Cutting blade
- Glue gun and glue sticks
- Glue stick
- Pencil and ruler

NOTE
The sizes of paper towel and toilet paper tubes may differ according to brand. Sometimes toilet paper rolls will fit inside paper towel tubes, sometimes on the outside. Adapt the instructions accordingly.

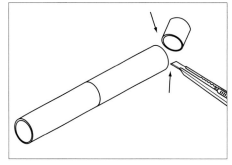

1 Insert the paper towel tube into both of the toilet paper tubes. Cut off the excess paper towel tube at one end.

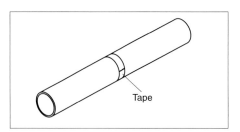

2 Tape the seam that joins the two toilet paper tubes.

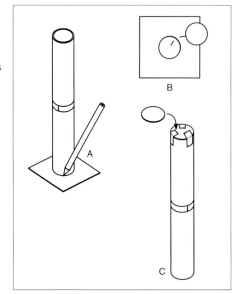

3 Place the tube on the 2 1/2" x 2 1/2" cardboard square (A) and trace around the base. Cut out the circle (B), making it a little smaller in order to fit at one end of the tube. Do not push the cardboard in too far. Level it off and then tape it to the tube (C).

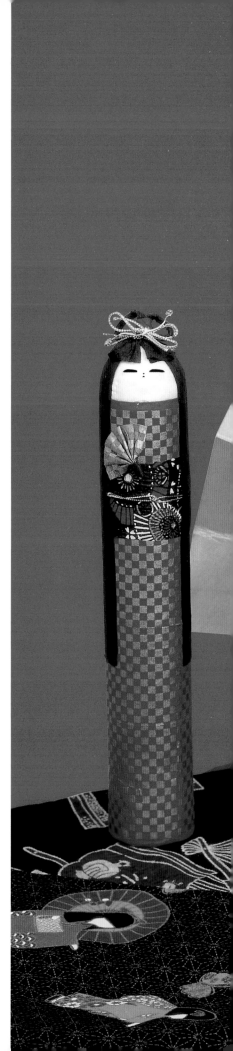

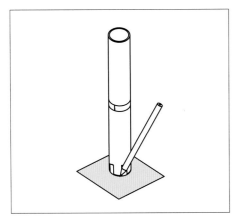

4 Take the 21/2" x 21/2" solid Washi square. Center the taped end of the tube on the square and trace around the bottom of the tube on the piece of solid Washi.

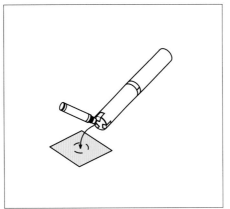

5 Apply the glue stick to the bottom of the taped tube and then place the tube on the solid Washi square. Make sure that it is centered on the square.

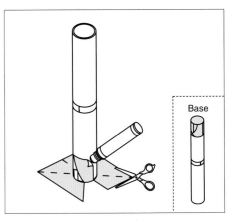

6 Snip the solid Washi into sections. Spread glue on the sections and smooth up the sides of the tube. Turn the tube over and leave to dry. This will be the base for the doll.

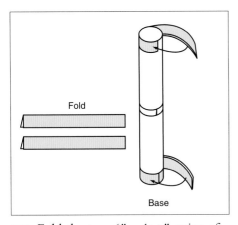

7 Fold the two 6" x 11/2" strips of solid Washi in half lengthwise. Paste down. Glue one strip around the neck of the tube, fold side up, and the other strip around the base, fold side down.

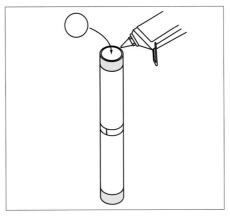

8 Heat the glue gun. With the base on the working surface, apply hot glue around the open-ended inside edge (neck) at the top of the tube. Insert the styrofoam ball into the opening before the glue dries.

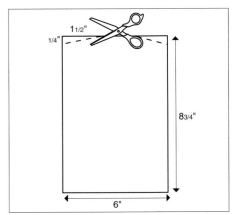

9 Cut out the printed Washi for the doll's kimono following the dimensions given. Cut off a small triangle on both corners of the paper. This will be placed at the neck of the kimono.

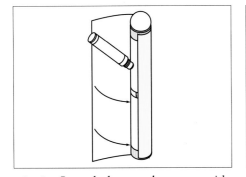

10 Spread glue on the wrong side of the printed Washi. Place one end 1/2" to the left of the center front and roll it around the tube. Small sections of the solid Washi should show at the top and bottom.

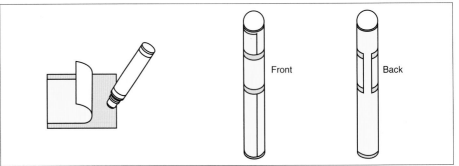

11 To make the obi (the broad sash which is tied in a large, flat bow at the back of a kimono), use the 6" x 13/4" rectangle of crimped printed Washi and the 6" x 2" rectangle of solid Washi. Take both obi pieces and paste the crimped Washi evenly on top of the solid Washi. Glue the Washi obi around the body of the doll, 11/2" below the neck, making sure that the Washi meets in the center at the back.

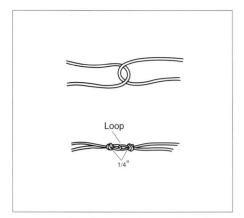

12 Take the two 8" lengths of cord. Fold them in half and then pass them through each other so that they meet at the looped ends. Make a knot in each end, 1/4" from the center where the loops meet.

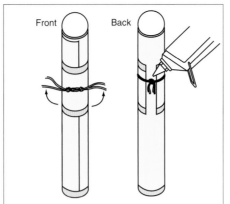

13 Center the loop and knots in front of the obi. Tie a small knot in the center back of the obi, snipping off any excess cord. Add a small amount of glue to the back to keep the knot in place.

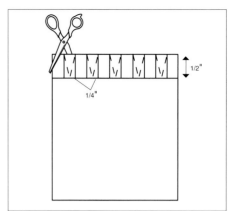

14 For the hair, take the 7" x 4" crimped black solid Washi. Make sure that the grain of the crimps is vertical. Cut out five triangles 1/2" deep and 1/4" wide, as shown in the diagram above.

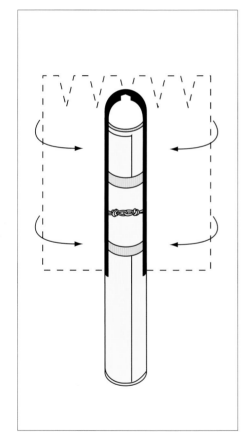

15 Before applying the glue stick to the doll, place the hair on the doll so you can judge where the glue needs to go. The triangles that you have cut out will help place the hair on top of the head without leaving too much bulk. Apply glue to the top, sides and back of the doll. Press the crimped Washi down.

16 To prepare the bangs and bow for the top of the doll's head, take the 5" x 1 1/2" piece of crimped solid Washi and fold it in thirds lengthwise.

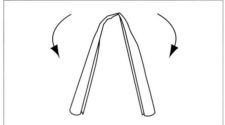

17 Then fold it in half length wise. Pinch the paper in the center.

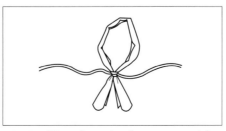

18 Tie a knot in the center with the 7" gold or silver cord.

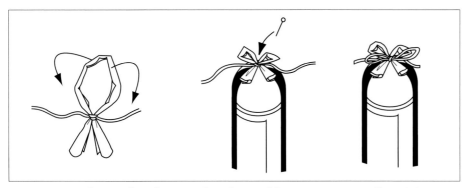

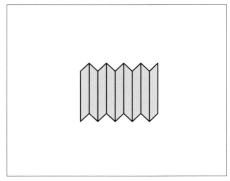

19 Turn the top hair loop under the cord knot. Insert a small straight pin to hold the hair in place. Carefully spread out the bangs and tie a bow with the cord. Use the hot glue gun to secure the bow in place.

21 Complete your doll by adding a little fan! Take the 1 1/2" x 1" gold Washi and fold lengthwise.

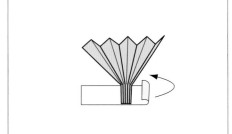

20 Finish off the doll's face by giving her some eyes, a nose and a little mouth. Use the fine-tipped black marker for the eyes and the fine-tipped red marker for the nose and mouth. Look at the samples above and decide which one you like. For some rosy cheeks, use the cutting blade to scrape off some red coloring pencil shavings. Dip the cotton ball into the shavings and rub on the cheeks of the doll.

22 Tie the bottom of the fan with the gold cord or use a remnant of solid Washi to hold it together. Paste the fan to the doll with the hot glue gun. The fan can be placed anywhere you choose!

Rosebuds

Roses are a universal symbol of love. A single handmade Washi rosebud or a mass of colorful Washi rosebuds make perfect gifts for Mother's Day and Valentine's Day but can be given at any time of the year as a token of love and friendship. Arranged in a single vase or as a spectacular centerpiece for a dining table, they can form a stylish accessory to any home. This craft idea is simple enough for children to make and is also an ideal craft item for bazaars!

EQUIPMENT AND MATERIALS FOR ONE ROSEBUD

- 1 square of printed Washi (6" x 6")
- 1 bamboo skewer (12")
- 2 large rose leaves (2")
- Roll of green florist's tape
- Small sharp scissors
- Water-based shellac (optional)

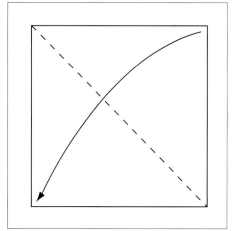

1 Take the 6" x 6" square of printed Washi.

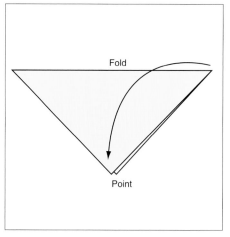

2 Fold the square of printed Washi into a triangle.

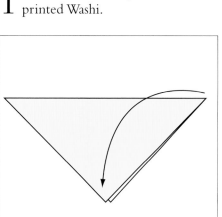

3 Hold the triangle with the fold side on top and the two points together. Start rolling the right-hand side of the triangle towards the center.

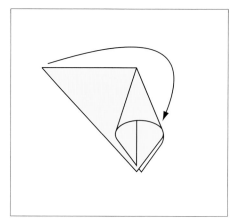

4 Loosely hold on to the points of the rolled triangle. Then roll the left-hand side towards the points to form a cone.

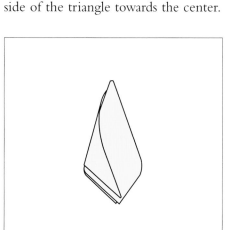

5 Do not worry if the folded rosebud looks a little loose. When it is gathered up, it will look fine!

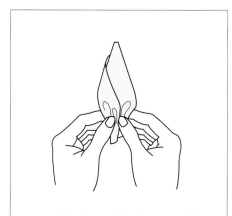

6 Holding the rosebud in both hands, carefully gather the cone bottom. Try not to lose the shape.

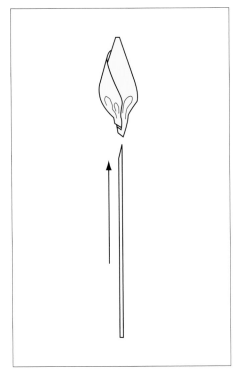 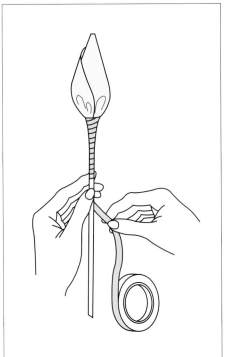 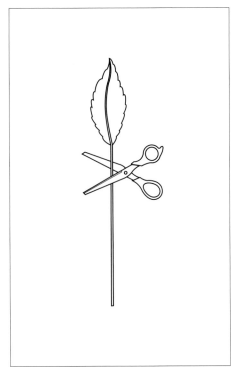

7 Hold the rosebud loosely in one hand. Carefully insert the pointed end of the bamboo skewer into the bottom center gathers of the rosebud.

8 Twist florist's tape at the top of the bamboo skewer to keep the bud in place. Continue twisting until the skewer is completely covered.

9 At the bottom of the skewer, go under, then twist back up about 1 1/2". Trim off some of the rose leaf stem. It should be about 1" long.

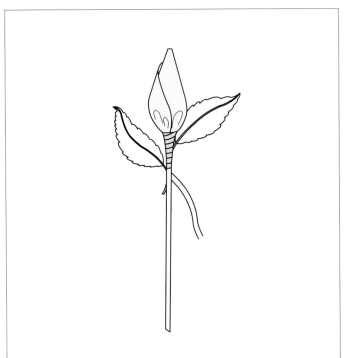 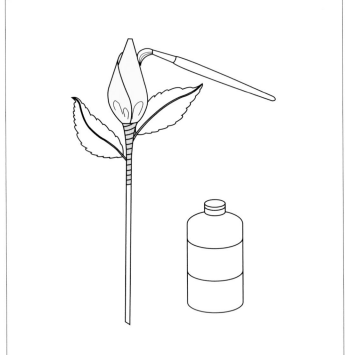

10 Add one rose leaf at a time. Place the first leaf under the rosebud with the leaf stem down the side of the skewer. Twist the florist's tape a few times around the covered skewer, gathering the leaf stem directly under the leaf. Continue until you reach the bottom of the leaf stem.

11 Place the second leaf on the opposite side of the skewer and secure with florist's tape. Continue down until the stem of the second leaf is completely covered. Shape the leaves so that they point outward. Complete the rosebud by brushing on some shellac to give it a little shine.

Oriental Roses

Roses – that most traditional of flowers – are appropriate for any occasion. By simply adding petals, the rosebuds on page 13 are transformed into stylish, full-blown flowers. They can be made in colors to suit the occasion, the time of the year, the location, and the message. Elegantly grouped with rosebuds in an Oriental vase (page 22) or arranged in a bowl or basket (page 70), these softly rounded Washi roses make a charming gift or decoration for the home.

EQUIPMENT AND MATERIALS FOR ONE ORIENTAL ROSE

- 1 rectangle of printed Washi (6 1/2" x 17")
- 1 rectangle of solid Washi (6 1/2" x 17")
- 1 square of printed Washi (4" x 4")
- 1 square of solid Washi (4" x 4")
- 1 bamboo skewer (12")
- 2 fabric rose leaves (2")
- 3 flower stamens
- Roll of green or brown florist's tape
- Florist's wire
- Tracing paper and pencil
- Ruler
- Small sharp scissors
- Paper clips
- Glue stick

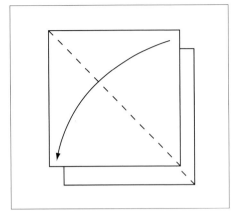

1 To make the central cone, take the 4" x 4" square of printed Washi and the 4" x 4" square of solid Washi.

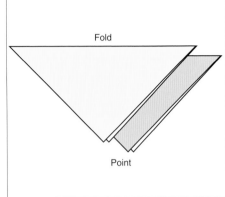

2 Fold the square pieces of printed and solid Washi into separate triangles.

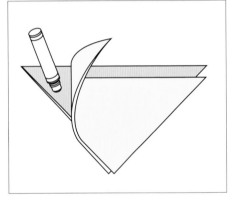

3 Place the printed Washi triangle on top of the solid one. Move the printed Washi down so that 1/4" of the solid Washi shows on the fold side. Paste together using the glue stick, then turn over.

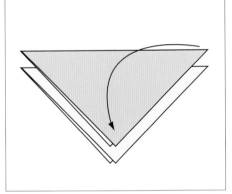

4 Hold the triangle with the fold side on top and the two points together. Start rolling the right-hand side of the triangle towards the center.

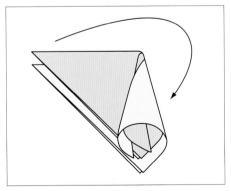

5 Loosely hold on to the points of the rolled triangle. Then roll the left-hand side towards the points to form a cone.

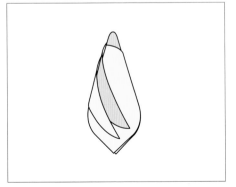

6 Do not worry if the folded rosebud looks a little loose. When it is gathered up, it will look fine!

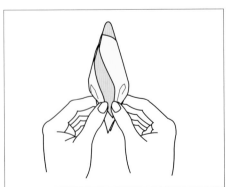

7 Holding the rosebud in both hands, carefully gather the cone bottom. Try not to lose the shape.

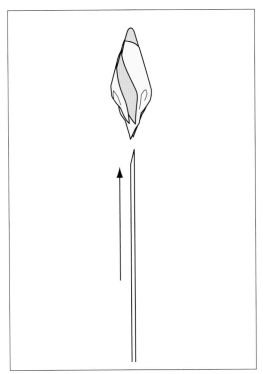

8 Hold the rosebud loosely in one hand. Carefully insert the pointed end of the bamboo skewer into the bottom center gathers of the rosebud.

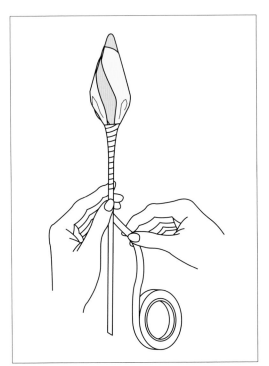

9 Twist florist's tape at the top of the bamboo skewer to keep the rosebud in place. Continue stretching and twisting the tape until it is halfway down the skewer.

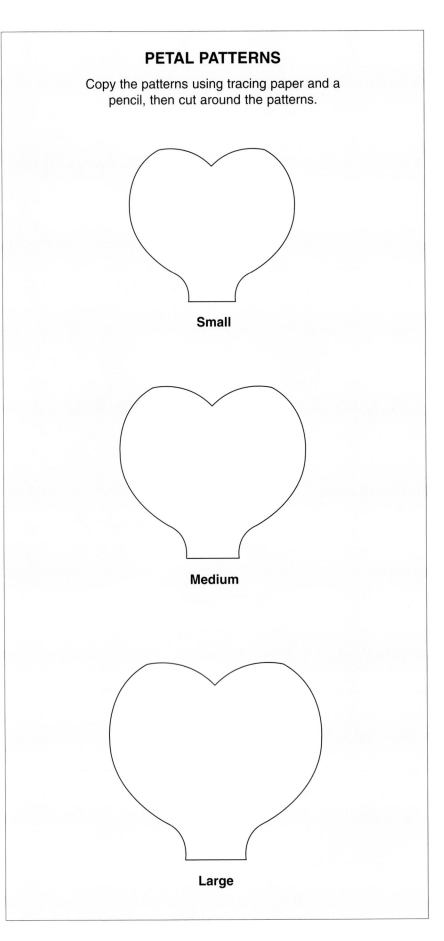

PETAL PATTERNS

Copy the patterns using tracing paper and a pencil, then cut around the patterns.

Small

Medium

Large

MAKING THE PETALS

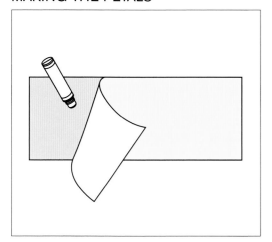

10 Paste the 6½" x 17" printed and solid Washi rectangles together using the glue stick.

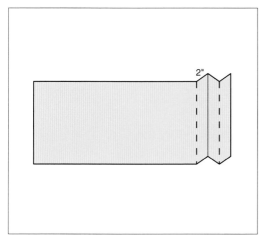

11 With the solid Washi side facing upward, fan-fold the combined papers every 2".

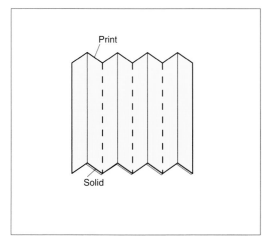

12 Continue folding all the way to the other end. When complete, there should be seven folds.

13 Trace and cut out the petal patterns on page 18. Place them on the fan-folded Washi with the ends of the petals toward the side that has four folds.

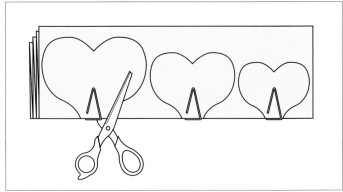

14 Secure the petal patterns with paper clips. Carefully cut around the patterns through all layers. When complete, there will be four folded petals of each size.

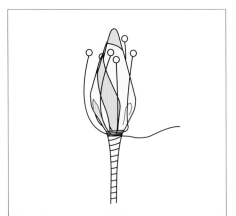

15 Go back to the rosebud. Twist a 12" strip of florist's wire around the base of the bud. Add the flower stamens around the base, securing them with the wire.

16 Add the rose petals, starting with the small, then the medium, then the large petals, by sliding the florist's wire between the folds of the petals.

17 Carefully gather each petal at the base, then secure with the wire. Whenever necessary, twist the wire all around the base to keep the petals in place. Continue adding petals.

18 When all the petals are in place, twist the remainder of the wire around the bamboo skewer a few times. If there is too much wire left, trim off the excess.

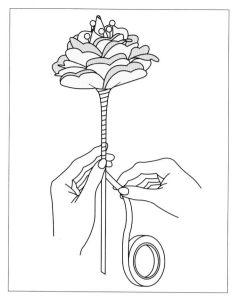

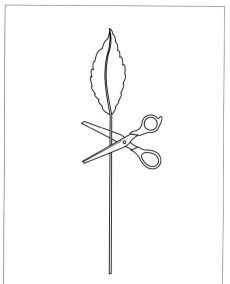

19 Twist florist's tape four or five times around the base of the rose until it looks smooth. Continue stretching and winding the tape down the bamboo skewer until it is completely covered. At the bottom of the skewer, go under, then twist the tape back up about 2".

20 Trim the stems of the leaves to 1", then add the leaves one at a time. Place the first leaf under the rose with the stem down the side of the skewer. Twist the florist's tape a few times around the skewer, gathering the leaf stem directly under the leaf. Continue to the bottom of the stem.

21 Place the second leaf on the opposite side of the skewer and secure with florist's tape, Continue twisting and stretching the tape until the stem of the second leaf is completely covered. Finish off the rose by shaping the leaves and petals, curving them outward.

Oriental Vase

This cleverly designed Washi vase – a charming alternative to a store-bought vase – makes a wonderful gift by itself or filled with Washi rosebuds (page 13) or Oriental roses (page 16)! The color of the vase can echo the tones of the flowers or be in a boldly contrasting shade. Too tall for a dinner party decoration, this flower-filled vase would make an eye-catching centerpiece for a buffet meal or could stand alone at eye level on a tall console table. Flowers can be arranged upright in the vase or gathered closely so that their heads peep over the edge.

EQUIPMENT AND MATERIALS FOR ONE ORIENTAL VASE

- 3 large 1/2 gallon milk cartons, washed and dried
- 3 printed Washi rectangles (4" x 83/4") for teardrop pattern
- 3 printed Washi rectangles (5" x 81/2") for triangle pattern
- 1 printed Washi square (31/4 x 31/4") for bottom of base
- 1 printed Washi strip (61/2" x 2") for around neck
- Transparent (Scotch) tape
- Tracing paper and pencil
- Thin cardboard
- Small sharp scissors
- Cutting blade
- Awl
- Ruler or measuring tape
- Large glue stick

PREPARING CARTON 1

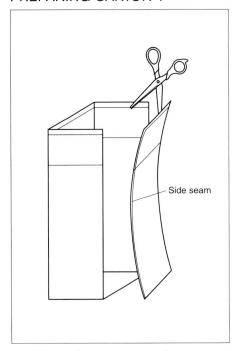

1 Using the scissors, cut down two sides of the milk carton and across the bottom. Make sure that one of the sides contains the seam.

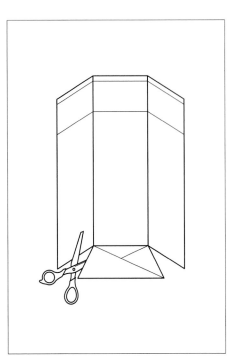

2 Cut the two adjacent sides of the milk carton so that only the middle section is connected to the bottom.

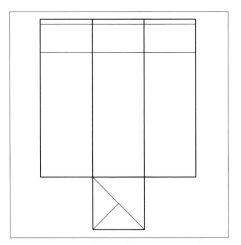

3 Open up the milk carton and lay it flat, on the table.

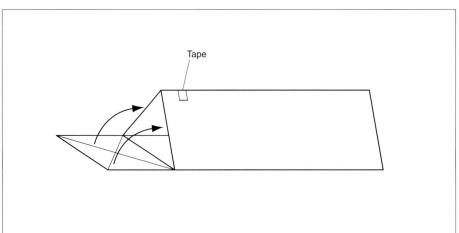

4 Pull the two sides not connected to the bottom together to form a triangular tube. Secure with a piece of tape. Pull the square bottom piece upward towards the tube.

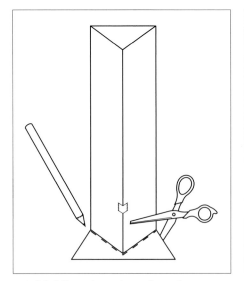

5 Holding the triangular tube upright, mark each side of the triangle on the square bottom. Cut off the excess carton on each side.

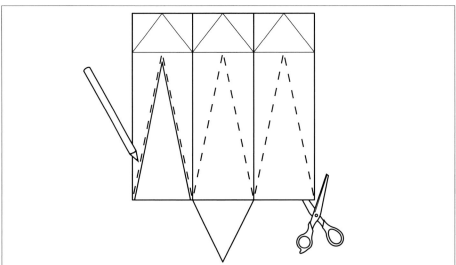

6 Remove the tape. Open the triangular tube and lay it flat with the outside facing upward. Using the triangle template on page 25, draw triangles on each side of the carton.

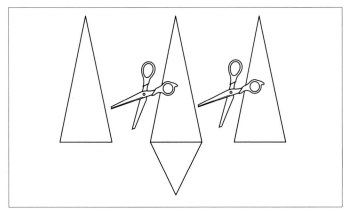

7 Cut out the two triangular sides to the left and right, leaving only the central section attached to the triangular bottom.

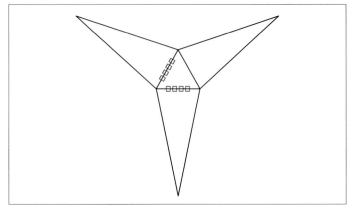

8 Tape the two triangular sections to the base triangle. Turn over and tape the seams on the other side. Use the cutting blade to level out both sides of the center triangle.

TRIANGLE TEMPLATE

Copy the template using tracing paper and a pencil.
Place the tracing on cardboard and draw
over the lines. Press heavily.
Cut out the template.

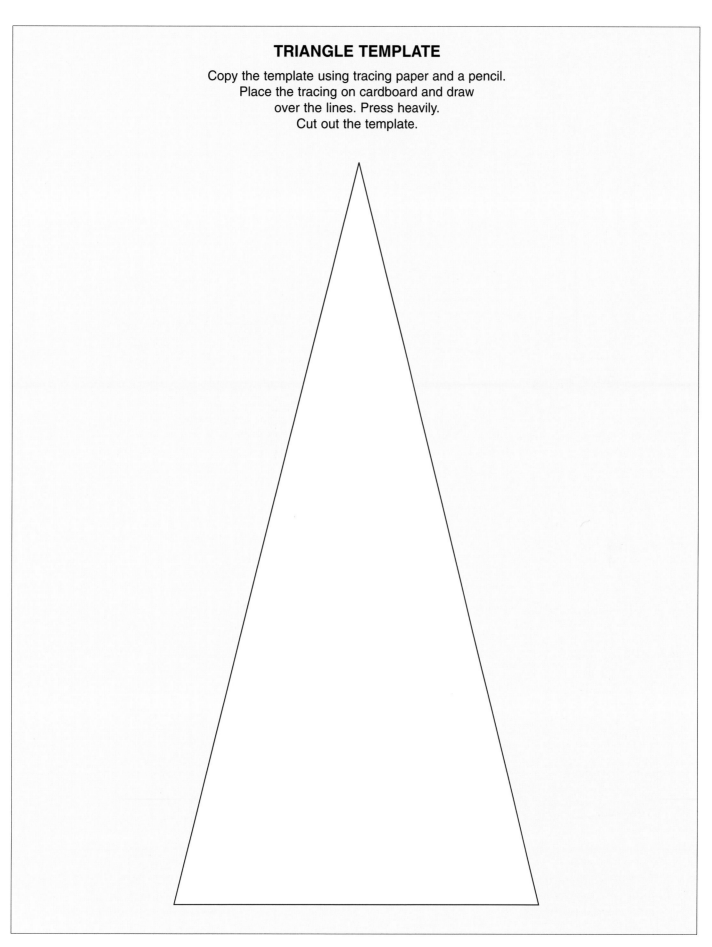

PREPARING CARTON 2

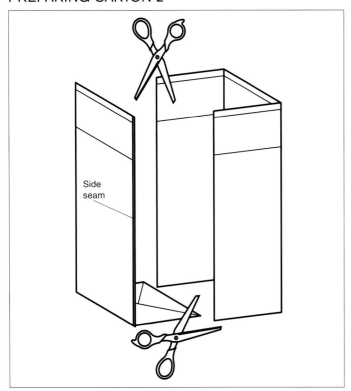

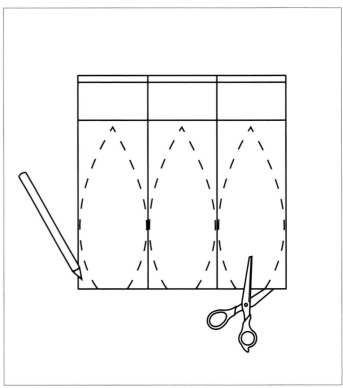

9 Using the scissors, cut down two sides of the milk carton, making sure that one of the sides contains the seam. Then cut away the bottom of the carton.

10 Open up the milk carton and lay it flat. Using the teardrop template on page 27, draw teardrops on each section of the carton. Cut out each teardrop section.

ASSEMBLING THE VASE

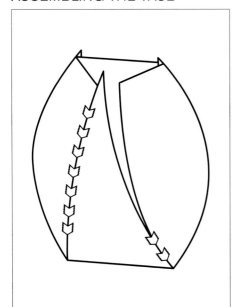

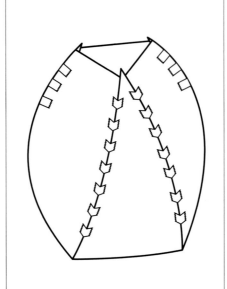

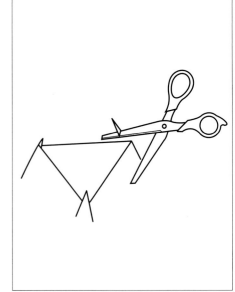

11 Tape the teardrop-shaped pieces of carton, with the points facing downward (carton 2), to the triangular base (carton 1).

12 Tape securely along the seams, working up from the bottom. Use 1" tape at the bottom and top and 2"-long tape in the middle.

13 Once the sides have been taped, trim off any extra carton at the top of the triangles, if necessary.

TEARDROP TEMPLATE

Copy the template using tracing paper and a pencil.
Place the tracing on cardboard and draw over the lines.
Press heavily. Cut out the template.

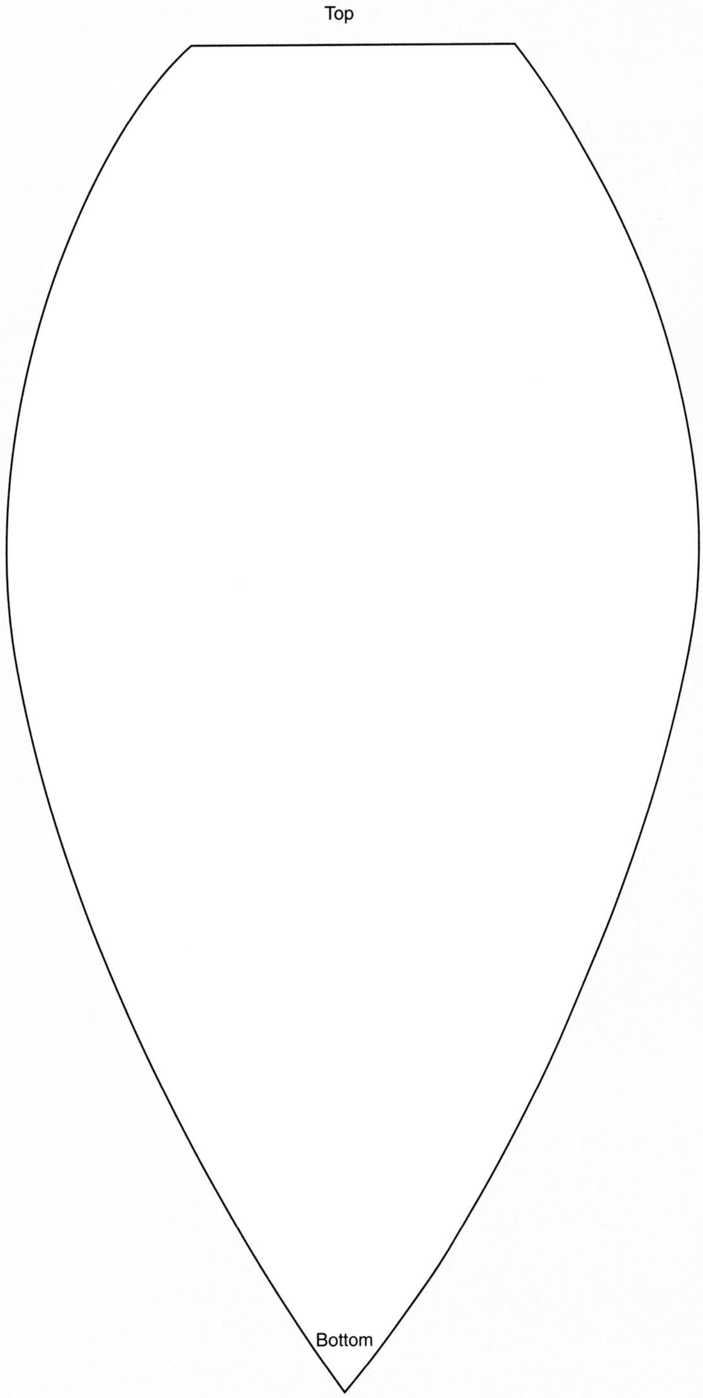

Top

Bottom

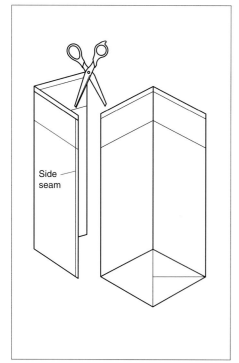

14 Using the scissors, cut the edges of the milk carton so that two sides are left attached to each other, while the other two remain attached to the bottom.

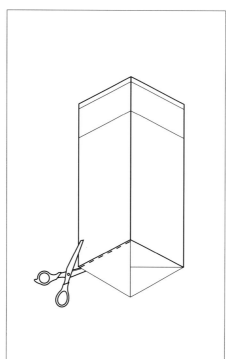

15 On the two sides that are attached to the bottom, cut along one of the short sides joining the side to the bottom.

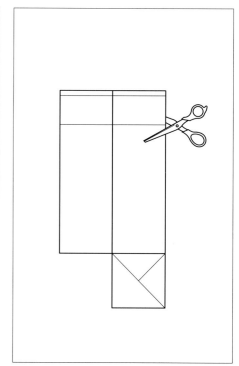

16 Open up the carton and lay it flat. Cut off the top part at the natural crease line where the carton is folded to form a spout.

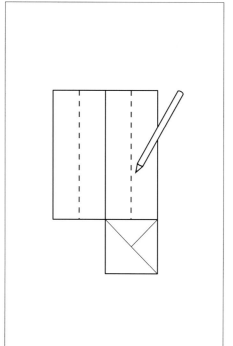

17 Turn the carton over so that the inside is facing upwards. Mark a line down the center of both sections with a pencil and ruler.

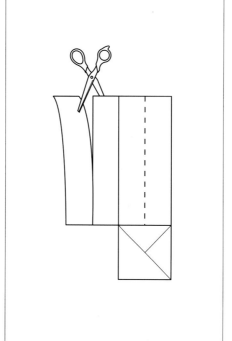

18 Cut off half of the divided portion that is not attached to the bottom square of the carton.

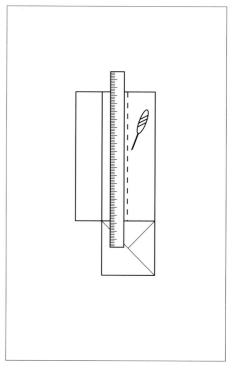

19 In the center of the section attached to the bottom square, make a crease with the awl or end of the scissors on top of the pencil line.

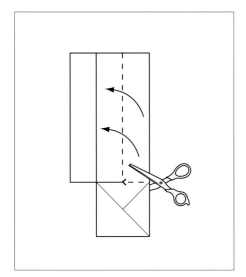

20 Cut halfway along the crease joining the section attached to the bottom square. Be careful not to cut in too far. Fold crease line to the left.

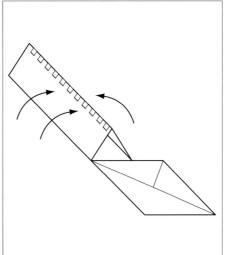

21 Turn the milk carton so that the outside is facing upward. Pull the two opposite sides towards the center to form a triangular tube. Tape along the seam.

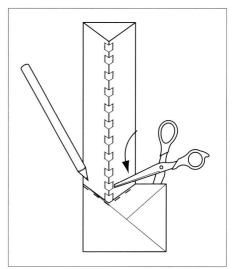

22 Holding the triangular tube upright, mark each side of the triangle on the square bottom. Cut off the excess carton.

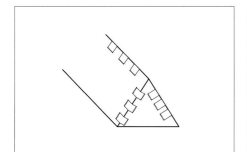

23 Tape the triangle to the tube. This is the end that will be inserted into the assembled vase.

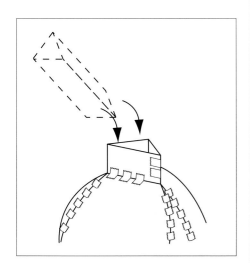

24 Insert the triangular tube into the assembled vase. Tape the neck to the vase around the edges.

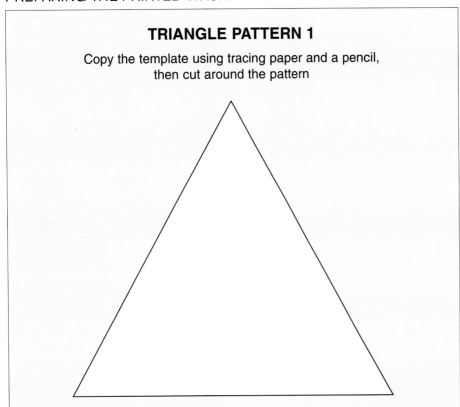

TRIANGLE PATTERN 1

Copy the template using tracing paper and a pencil,
then cut around the pattern

25 Trace and cut the following pieces out of the printed Washi using the triangle patterns (left) and on page 32 and the teardrop pattern on page 31:

- 1 triangle for the bottom
- 3 triangle patterns for the sides
- 3 teardrop patterns for the sides
- 1 strip (61/2" x 2") for the neck

TIP
If your printed Washi has a definite one-way design, make sure you place the patterns in the right direction before cutting out the Washi.

TEARDROP PATTERN

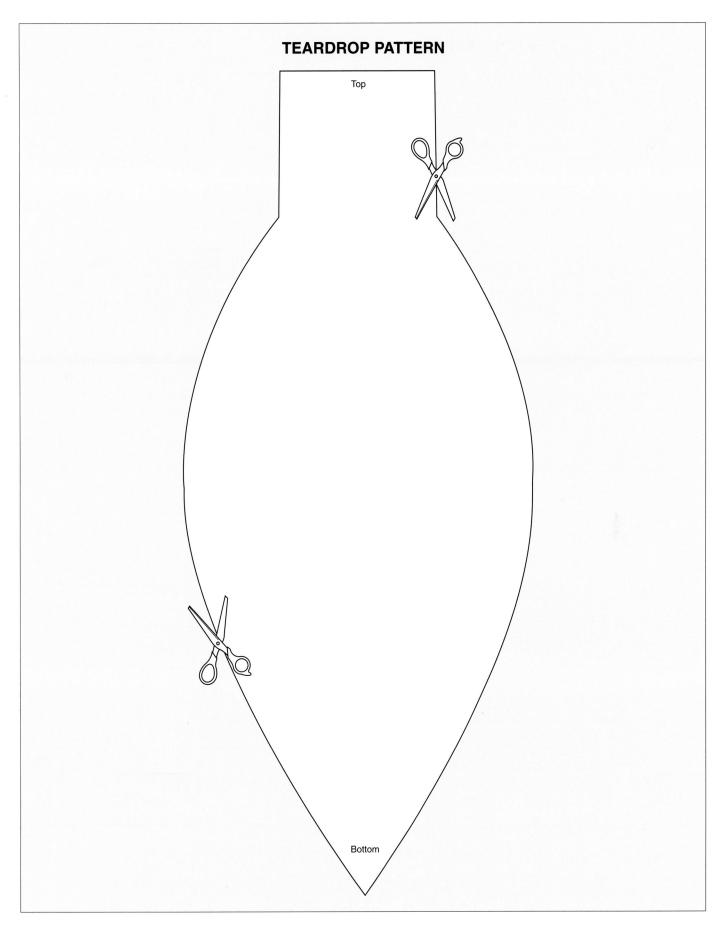

Top

Bottom

TRIANGLE PATTERN 2

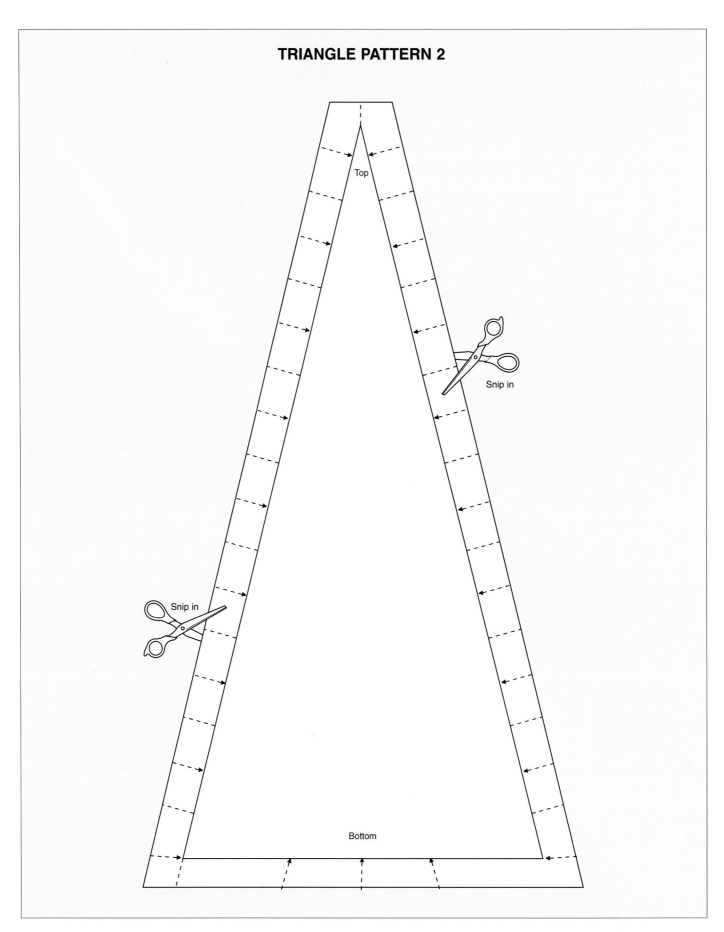

Top

Snip in

Snip in

Bottom

APPLYING THE WASHI

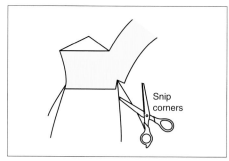

Snip corners

26 Using a large glue stick, paste the long strip of printed Washi around the neck of the vase.

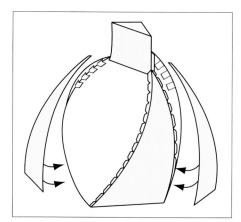

27 Apply glue stick to the wrong side of the three triangular pieces of Washi. Paste to the milk carton starting from the top. Turn under 1/2" at the bottom. Smooth out the snipped edges where they overlap the seams.

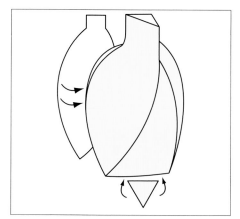

28 Next, apply glue stick to the wrong side of the teardrop pieces of Washi. Starting at the bottom, smooth out until you get to the top. At the top, fold 1/2" of Washi inside the opening. Paste the Washi triangle to the bottom of the vase.

Cherry Blossom Box in Two Sizes

Ｏne of the many Japanese creative crafts made from milk cartons, this wonderful little box takes its name from the cherry blossom which it resembles. The box makes a lovely gift by itself or it can be filled with a surprise! It is also great as a candy container or jewelry box!

EQUIPMENT AND MATERIALS FOR ONE BOX

- 1 large (1/2 gallon) or small (1 quart) milk carton, washed and dried
- 1/3 sheet of printed Washi for the large milk carton
- 1/8 sheet of printed Washi for the small milk carton
- 1 piece of cardboard (10" x 10" x 1/4")
- 1 wooden bead with a large hole in the center, if desired
- Cord (8" x 1/4") (16" x 1/4" for a double knot)
- Transparent (Scotch) tape
- Small sharp scissors
- Cutting blade
- Awl
- Ruler and pencil
- Hot glue gun and glue sticks
- Large glue stick

PREPARING THE PRINTED WASHI AND CARDBOARD

Printed Washi Large (gallon)	Small (quart)
• 1 rectangle (16" x 6")	• 1 rectangle (12" x 6")
• 2 squares (31/2" x 31/2")	• 2 squares (21/2" x 21/2")
• 1 square (51/2" x 51/2")	• 1 square (41/2" x 41/2")
• 1 square (71/2" x 71/2")	• 1 square (51/2" x 51/2")

Cardboard Large (gallon)	Small (quart)
• 1 square (31/2" x 31/2")	• 1 square (21/2" x 21/2")
• 1 square (41/2" x 41/2")	• 1 square (31/2" x 31/2")

1 Decide which size box you want to make and cut out the relevant patterns from the printed Washi and cardboard.

MAKING THE LID

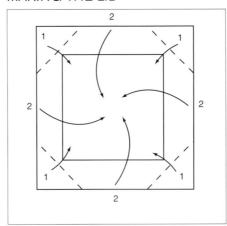

2 With the glue stick, paste the appropriate piece of printed Washi to the correct size cardboard (71/2" x 71/2" Washi to the 41/2" x 41/2" cardboard; 51/5" x 51/2" Washi to the 31/2" x 31/2" cardboard). Glue down opposing sides 1 first. Then glue down sides 2.

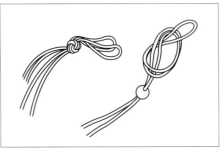

3 Make a handle by knotting the cord near the top. Alternatively, use a wooden bead to form a handle.

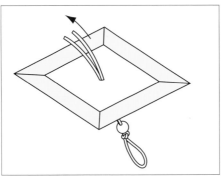

4 Using the awl or the point of the scissors, make a hole in the center of the larger piece of cardboard. Decide on the knot you want. Pull the loose ends of the cord through the hole.

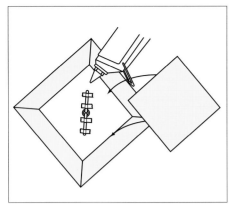

5 Tape the loose pieces of cord to the cardboard. Hot glue the unfinished sides of the cardboard together, centering them. Leave the lid to dry.

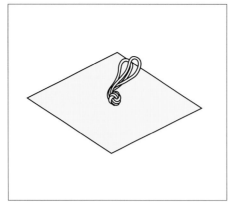

6 The top of the lid with a bead handle will look like this.

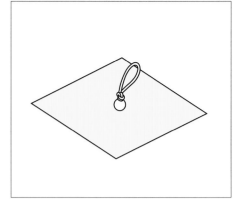

7 The top of the lid with the knot handle will look like this.

MAKING THE BOX

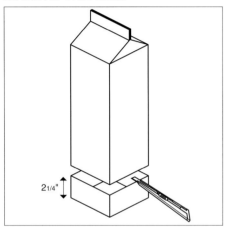

8 Measure 2¼" up the side of the milk carton (large or small) and mark all round. Cut off the bottom with the cutting blade.

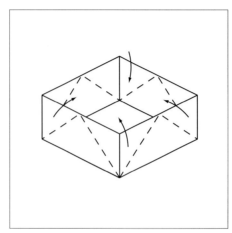

9 Using the awl, score lines from the top middle to the bottom corners on each side of the carton.

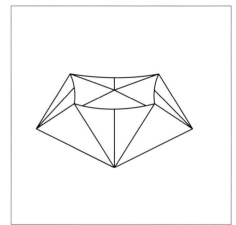

10 Push the corners of the carton in, along the scored lines, to form additional sides.

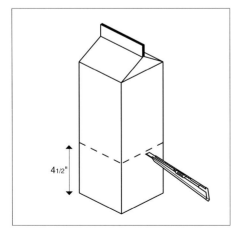

11 Measure 4½" up the side of the carton and mark all round. Cut around the carton with the blade.

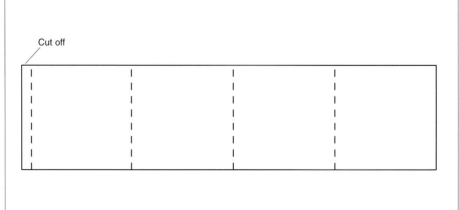

12 Find the seamed side of the carton. Carefully pull or cut the carton apart, then cut off the extra flap.

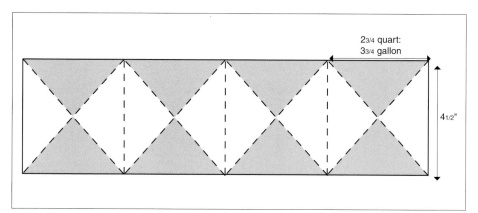

13 Lay the middle section of the carton flat with the inside facing upwards. Draw diagonal lines between the naturally folded corners of the carton. Cut along the drawn lines. Keep only the shaded pieces.

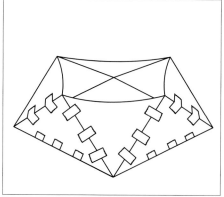

14 Tape the eight pieces, wrong side facing out, to the eight-sided bottom outside sections. Carefully seal all the edges with tape.

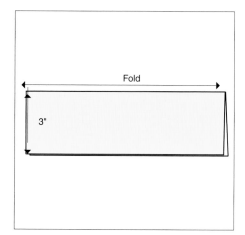

15 Fold the printed Washi rectangle in half lengthwise. Open up. On the wrong side of the Washi, pencil in the crease line.

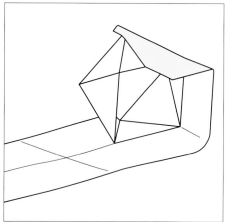

16 Spread glue on each triangle. Line up the upper edge of the box on the penciled line, then roll each side of the box on to the Washi.

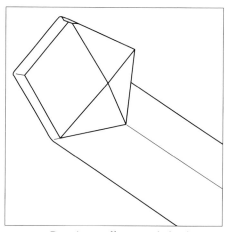

17 Continue all around the box. Smooth out any wrinkles in the Washi that appear on the sides of the box.

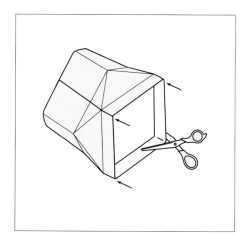

18 Clip the overhang at the bottom of the box. Clip at an angle from the outside corner to the inside corner.

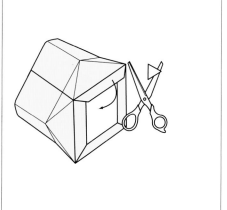

19 Glue the opposite sides down. Fold and cut the remaining corners at a 45° angle, then glue them to the bottom of the carton.

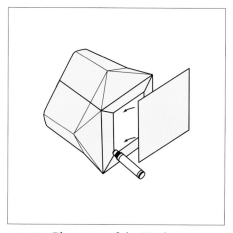

20 Glue one of the Washi squares (3 1/2" x 3 1/2" or 2 1/2" x 2 1/2") to the bottom of the box to hide the folds and neaten the bottom.

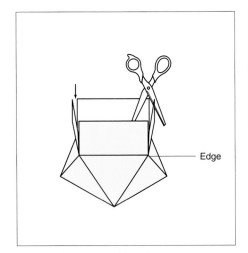

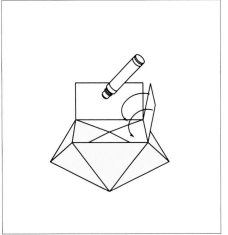

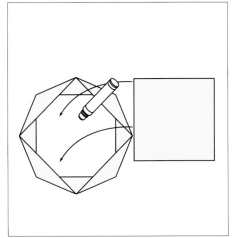

21 At each of the four corners of the box, cut the remaining pulled up Washi flaps down to the edge of the box.

22 Spread glue on the flaps, one at a time, then push them inside the box. Smooth out any bumps, folds or wrinkles.

23 Glue the second square of Washi (3 1/2" x 3 1/2" or 2 1/2" x 2 1/2") to the inside center of the box to neaten the inside.

Covered Boxes

In Japan, boxes of all shapes and sizes, made from a variety of materials, have long been used as storage containers and gift "wrappers". Boxes have particular aesthetic appeal to the Japanese and much effort goes into their decoration; the Japanese believe that the beauty of a wrapped gift is a reflection of the sincerity of the person giving the gift. Here is a great way to turn a small cardboard box into a pretty jewelry or gift box or a large, sturdy cardboard box into a useful storage container! The boxes can be decorated to suit the occasion or the age and interests of the recipient.

EQUIPMENT AND MATERIALS FOR ONE BOX

- Shallow cardboard box (square or rectangle, no more than 3" deep)
- Printed Washi (amount will depend on the size of the box)
- Large glue stick
- Hot glue gun and glue sticks
- Small sharp scissors
- Ruler or measuring tape
- Pencil and pad of paper
- Small flowers tied with a ribbon (optional)
- Washi (origami) crane (see pages 48–9) (optional)
- Water-based shellac (optional)

COVERING THE LID

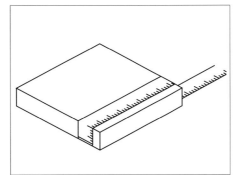

1 Measure the length of the lid from the bottom of one side, over the top and down to the bottom of the other side. Jot down the measurement and add 1 1/2" to it. This is the total length you will be working with. If your box is square, proceed to step 3 as the total length will be the same for both sides.

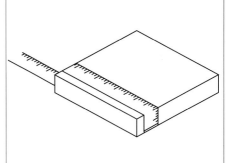

2 Measure the width of the lid from the bottom of one side, over the top and down to the bottom of the other side. Jot down the total measurement and add 1 1/2" to it. This is the total width you will be working with.

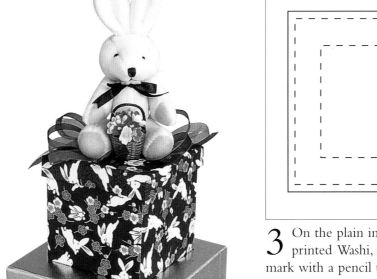

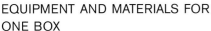

3 On the plain inside of the printed Washi, measure and mark with a pencil the rectangle/square measurements needed for your box lid. Cut out the rectangle/square of printed Washi.

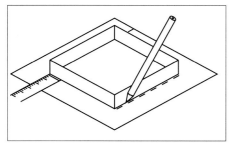

4 Place the box lid upside down in the center of the plain Washi. Draw a line around the lid. Use the ruler or tape measure to check that the seams are the same width on all four sides.

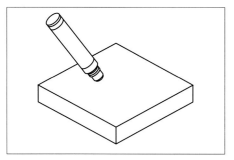

5 Leaving the Washi on the working surface, spread glue all over the top of the box lid.

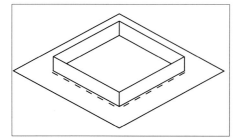

6 Place the lid back on the Washi making sure it is placed within the drawn lines. Turn the lid over and smooth out any wrinkles in the Washi.

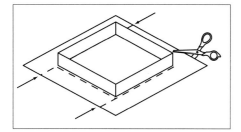

7 Draw lines from the outer edges of the Washi to the four corners of the lid. Cut along the lines up to the edges of the lid.

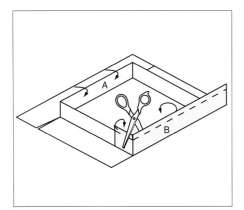

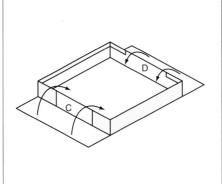

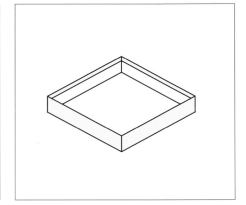

8 Spread glue on the Washi on sides A and B, then smooth the Washi up, around and over the sides of the lid. Cut down the corner seams from the top to the inside corner. Apply glue and fold over. Smooth down inside.

9 Repeat for sides C and D of the lid. Spread glue on the Washi flaps, fold up and over, and smooth down neatly inside the lid.

10 Allow the lid to dry completely before placing it on the bottom half of the box.

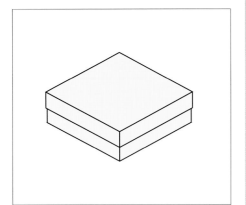

11 To cover the bottom half of the box, repeat steps 1–9. If the box is small, use printed Washi. If the box is large, it is best to use solid Washi as a contrast.

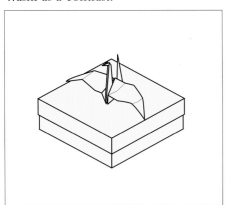

12 To complete the box, shellac the lid to give it a pretty shine. This will also help to preserve it. Add a Washi crane or small artificial flowers for decoration. Be creative!

Crane Pencil Holder and Pencil

This Washi pencil holder and pencil, whimsically decorated with Japanese origami cranes, makes an attractive and unusual accessory for an office or home study. It is an ideal Father's Day gift for a child to make.

EQUIPMENT AND MATERIALS FOR ONE CRANE PENCIL HOLDER AND PENCIL

Crane Pencil Holder
• 1 square of printed Washi (6" x 6")
• 1 square of printed Washi (5 1/2" x 5 1/2")
• 1 square of printed Washi (2 1/2" x 2 1/2") for the crane decoration
• 1 square of solid Washi (3" x 3")
• 2 squares of cardboard (3 1/2" x 3 1/2" x 1/4")
• 1 empty toilet paper roll
• 1 empty paper towel roll
• 1 piece of ribbon (15" x 1/4")
• 1 piece of ribbon (7" x 1/4")
• Glue stick
• Hot glue gun and glue sticks
• Transparent (Scotch) tape
• Small sharp scissors
• Cutting blade

Crane Pencil
• 1 standard unsharpened pencil without an eraser
• 1 rectangle of printed Washi (7" x 1 1/4")
• 1 square of printed Washi (2 1/2" x 2 1/2") for the crane decoration
• 1 piece of ribbon (7" x 1/4")
• Ruler

NOTE
The sizes of paper towel and toilet paper tubes may differ according to brand. Sometimes toilet paper rolls will fit inside paper towel tubes, sometimes on the outside. Adapt the instructions accordingly.

CRANE PENCIL HOLDER

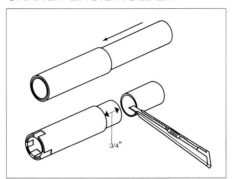

1 Insert the paper towel tube into the toilet paper tube and tape the end where they meet. Measure 3/4" up the other end, mark all around it, and cut off the excess paper towel tube.

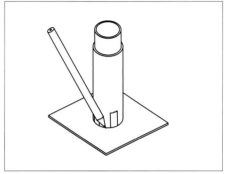

2 Place the tube in the center of one of the cardboard squares and trace around the outside.

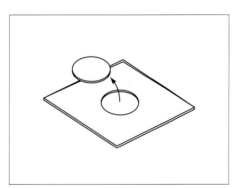

3 Cut out the traced circle with the cutting blade. Put the circle aside and return to the taped tube.

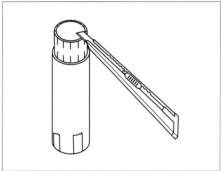

4 Use the scissors or cutting blade to snip the protruding paper towel tube at 1/4" intervals to where it meets the toilet paper tube.

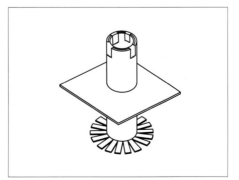

5 Spread out the 1/4" sections. Place the cut out cardboard square over the taped toilet paper tube and push it down to the bottom.

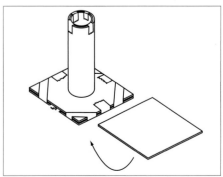

6 Place the second square of cardboard underneath the first piece and tape the sides of both pieces together.

44

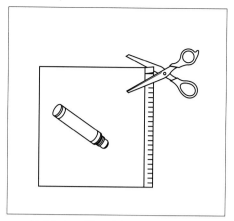

7 Fold the 6" x 6" square of printed Washi over 1/2" along one end. Make 1/2" cuts at 1/4" intervals along the fold. Spread glue on the wrong side of the printed Washi.

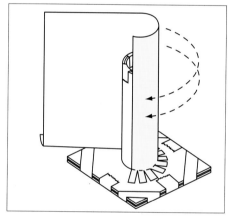

8 Paste the printed Washi around the tube, spreading the 1/4" sections out on the cardboard base.

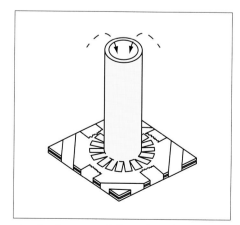

9 At the top of the tube, glue the excess printed Washi and fold it to the inside of the tube.

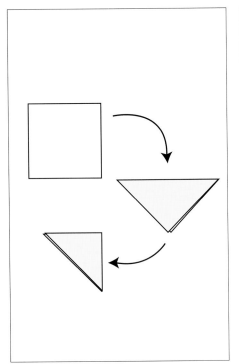

10 Take the 5½" x 5½" square of printed Washi. Fold it in half, then in half again to form a triangle. Crease all sides of the folded triangle.

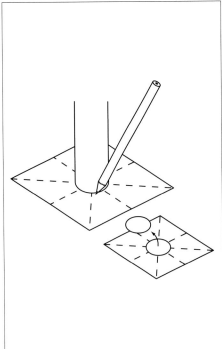

11 Open up the Washi square. Place the leftover piece of paper towel tube in the center of the Washi and draw around it. Cut out the circle with the cutting blade.

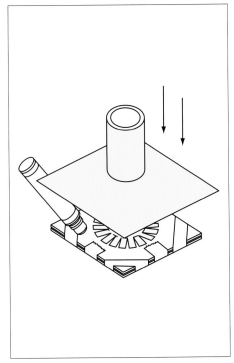

12 Spread glue on the cardboard square. Place the square of printed Washi over the top of the tube, push it to the bottom of the tube and smooth out any wrinkles.

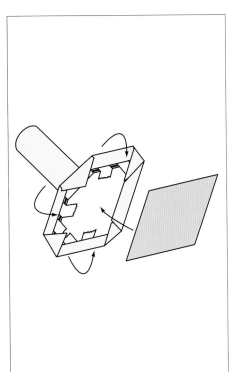

13 Turn the holder over. Tidy the base by gluing and folding over the sides of the Washi. Then glue the 3¼" x 3¼" square of solid Washi to the base to form a neat cover.

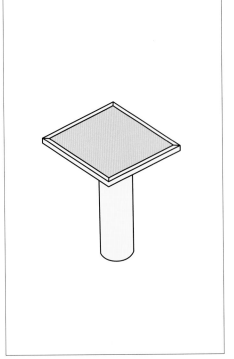

14 Turn the holder upside down and leave it until the base is completely dry.

CRANE PENCIL

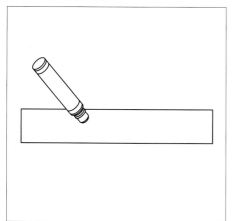

15 Take the 7" x 1 1/4" rectangle of printed Washi and spread glue all over the plain side.

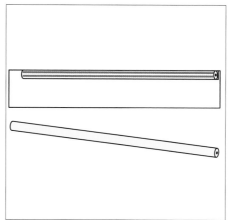

16 Place the pencil on one long side of the glued Washi and roll until it is covered with the Washi. Snip off any excess paper at the ends.

17 Tie the 7" x 1/4" ribbon into a small bow.

18 Glue the bow to the top of the pencil using the hot glue gun.

19 Then glue a Washi origami crane (see instructions on pages 48–9) on top of the bow.

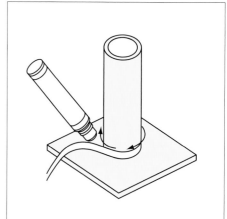

20 Spread glue on the wrong side of the second 7" x 1/4" ribbon and place it around the base of the pencil holder.

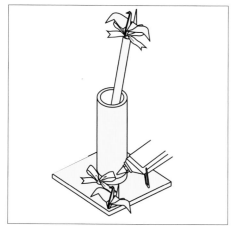

21 Glue a second bow and Washi origami crane on the ribbon of the pencil holder near the base.

WASHI ORIGAMI CRANE

TIP
Always hold and fold the Washi in the position shown in the diagrams.

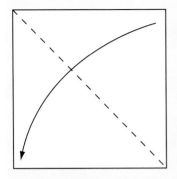

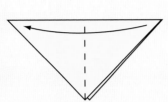

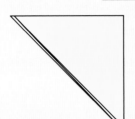

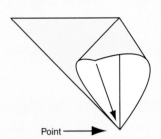

1. Place the 2½" x 2½" square of printed Washi wrong (plain) side up.

2. Fold in half.

3. Fold in half again.

4. Pull the point over to the right side.

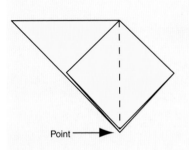

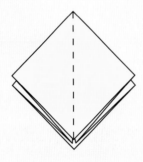

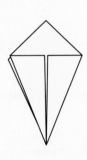

5. Bring the point down to form a square.

6. Repeat on the printed Washi side. Turn over and repeat.

7. Pull in the two sides.

8. Turn over and repeat.

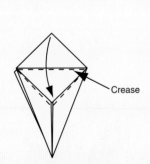

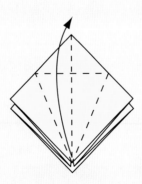

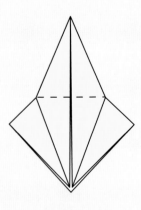

9. Fold the top down and crease, then pull back up.

10. Open the back up to form a square. Turn over and repeat.

11. Pull the point up, bringing sides to the center.

12. Crease and flatten out.

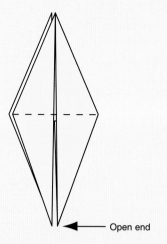

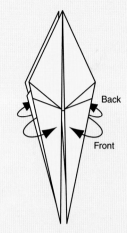

13. Turn over and repeat.

14. Fold in the two sides.

15. Turn over and repeat.

16. Pull in both sides on front and back.

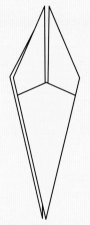

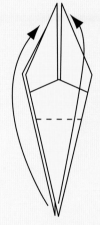

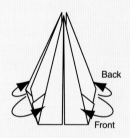

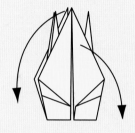

17. Turn over and repeat. The result should look like this.

18. Pull up both front and back point sections.

19. Fold the sections together on both the front and back.

20. The result should look like this.

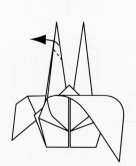

21. Pull the wings up and out. Bend one side down to form the head.

Obi Wall Hanging, Refrigerator Magnet and Ornament

In Japan, the traditional obi – the long, narrow piece of silk tied round the waist to keep a kimono in place – has become a popular item among Westerners for decorating their homes. This Washi interpretaion of the traditional obi, hung on a wall or door, will not only enhance your home but will also add Oriental character and atmosphere. Measurements and instructions are also given for making tiny obi refrigerator magnets and tree ornaments, but there are many other creative ways to incorporate the Washi obi into the home for different occasions.

EQUIPMENT AND MATERIALS FOR ONE FAN- OR BOW-STYLE OBI WALL HANGING, REFRIGERATOR MAGNET AND ORNAMENT

Obi Wall Hanging
- 1 full sheet (FS) of printed Washi (39" x 26")
- 1 half sheet (HS) of printed Washi (26" x 191/2")
- 1 full sheet (FS) piece of thin cardboard (23" x 7")
- 1 half sheet (HS) piece of thin cardboard (161/2" x 5")
- 1 wooden dowel (FS) (9" x 3/8")
- 1 wooden dowel (HS) (7" x 5/16")
- 1 length of cord (FS) for the dowel (15" x 1/8")
- 1 length of cord (HS) for the dowel (9" x 1/8")
- 2 plastic or wooden beads with (FS) 3/8" or (HS) 5/16" holes for the ends of the wooden dowel
- 1 length of solid colored cord (25" x 1/8") for tying

Obi Magnet or Ornament
- 1 piece of printed Washi (10" x 51/2")
- 1 wooden dowel (4" x 1/4")
- 2 plastic or wooden beads with 1/4" holes for the ends of the dowel
- 1 length of solid colored cord (10" x 1/8") for tying
- 1 length of solid colored cord (6" x 1/8") for the dowel
- 2 magnet strips (1")

For All Objects
- Small sharp scissors
- Ruler and pencil
- Small stapler for ornament magnet
- Glue stick
- Hot glue gun and glue sticks
- 2–4 clothes pins
- Flowers or additional beads for decoration

PREPARING THE WASHI

Fan- or bow-style obi magnet or ornament
1 rectangle (51/2" x 3")
3 rectangles (51/2" x 11/2")

Half sheet
Fan- or bow-style obi wall hanging
1 rectangle (191/2" x 11")
3 rectangles (191/2" x 5")

Full sheet
Fan- or bow-style obi wall hanging
1 rectangle (26" x 18")
3 rectangles (26" x 7")

1 Choose the size of the obi you want to make. Measure and cut out all the pieces in printed Washi. A visual sample of the layout is given below.

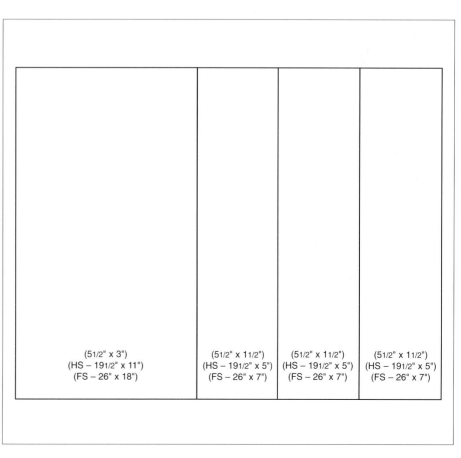

(51/2" x 3")
(HS – 191/2" x 11")
(FS – 26" x 18")

(51/2" x 11/2")
(HS – 191/2" x 5")
(FS – 26" x 7")

(51/2" x 11/2")
(HS – 191/2" x 5")
(FS – 26" x 7")

(51/2" x 11/2")
(HS – 191/2" x 5")
(FS – 26" x 7")

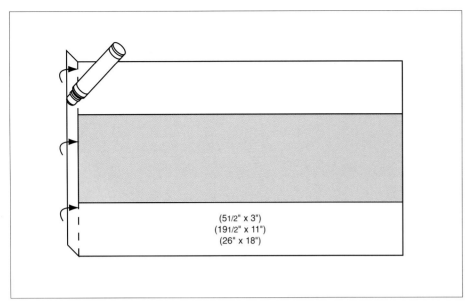

2 Center the cardboard on the largest piece of printed Washi and fold over 1/8" (HS/FS − 1/2") at one short end. Paste down using the glue stick.

(51/2" x 3")
(191/2" x 11")
(26" x 18")

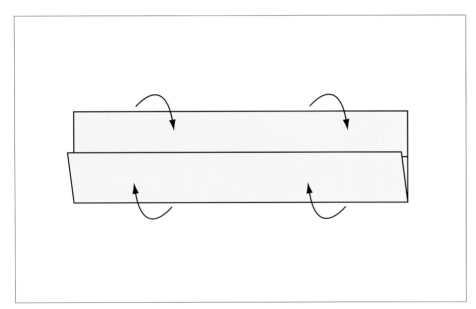

3 Fold the two long sides over the cardboard, overlapping them in the center.

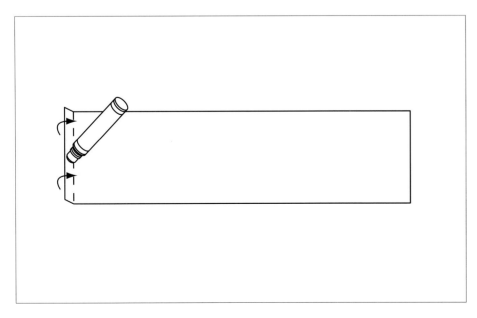

4 Take one of the three narrow strips of printed Washi (51/2" x 11/2") (HS − 191/2 x 5"; FS − 26" x 7") and fold over 1/4" (HS/FS − 1/2") on one short, narrow side. Paste down using the glue stick.

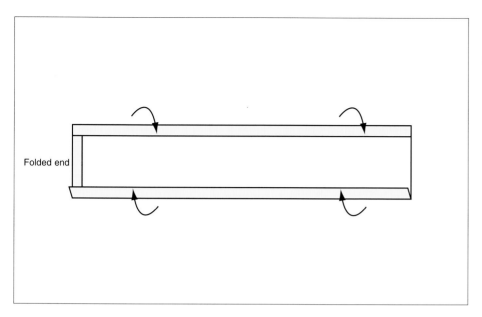

Folded end

5 Fold over the two long sides 1/8"
(HS/FS − 1/2") They should not
meet in the center.

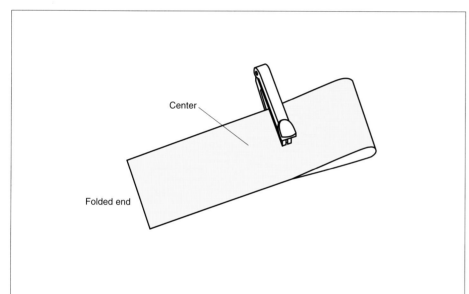

Center

Folded end

6 Fold the unfolded narrow end
over approximately 1/2" (HS − 2";
FS − 3 1/2") above the halfway point
and staple down.

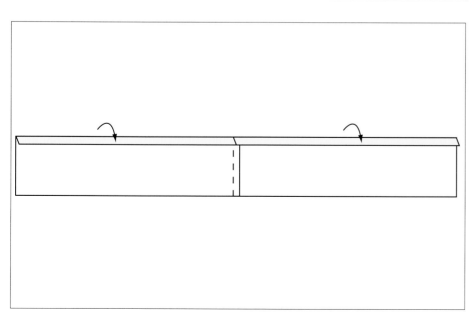

7 For the fan-style obi, take the
last two narrow strips of printed
Washi (5" x 1 1/2") (HS − 19 1/2" x 5";
FS − 26" x 7"). Overlap 1/4" (HS/FS −
1/2") at one end of each piece and
paste together. Fold over 1/4" (HS/
FS − 1/2") along the entire length and
paste down using the glue stick.

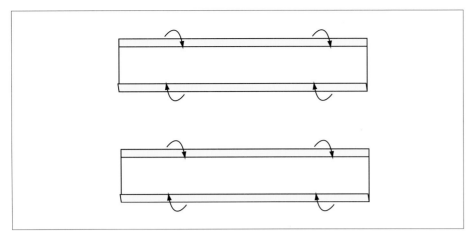

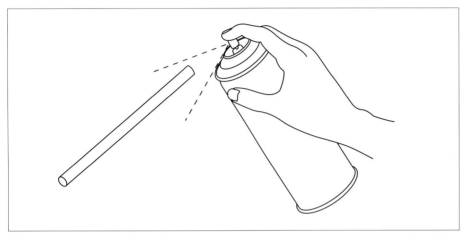

8 For the bow-style obi, take the last two narrow strips of printed Washi (5" x 1 1/2") (HS – 19 1/2" x 5"; FS – 26" x 7") and fold over 1/4" (HS/FS – 1/2") along both long sides. Paste down using the glue stick.

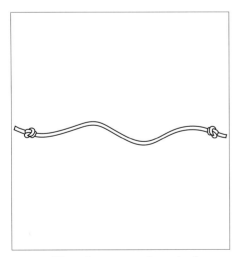

9 Cut the dowel to the appropriate length (4" x 1/4"; HS – 7" x 5/16"; FS – 9" x 3/8") and spray it with paint.

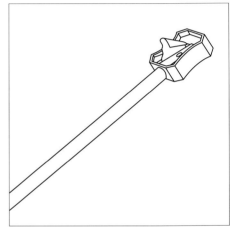

10 When dry, slightly sharpen each end of the dowel with a pencil sharpener.

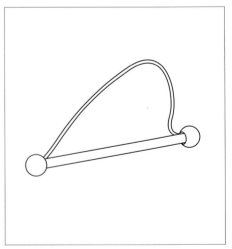

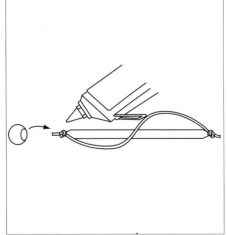

11 Tie a knot at each end of the cord (6" x 1/8"; HS – 9" x 1/8"; FS – 15" x 1/8").

12 Hot glue the knotted ends of the cord to each end of the dowel.

13 Hot glue wooden or plastic beads to each end of dowel to cover and secure the cord.

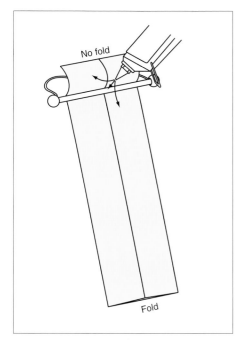

14 To assemble the obi, place the dowel at the unfolded end of the Washi, wrong side facing up. Pull 1" (HS − 2"; FS − 2 1/2") of the Washi through the cord, over the dowel and down the other side.

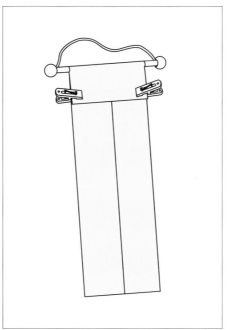

15 Center the Washi under the dowel. Apply hot glue inside the fold where the dowel and Washi meet. Fold over the end of the strip, glue and press down. Use clothes pins to seal the layers of Washi.

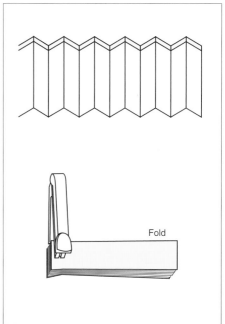

16 To make the fan, take the long, narrow strip which has a fold on one side (step 7, page 53) and fan-fold from one end to the other. To keep the fan in place, staple the long end without the fold.

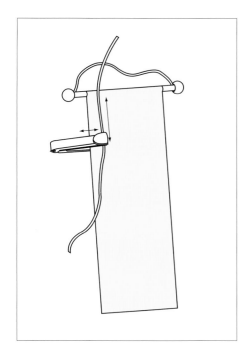

17 To assemble the fan-styled obi, fold the 10" (HS/FS− 25") length of cord in half. Staple it to the Washi strip 1" (HS − 4"; FS − 5 1/2") below the left side of the dowel and 1/2" (HS − 1 1/2"; FS − 2 1/2") in from the side.

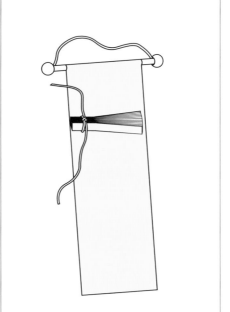

18 Center the fan horizontally over the cord. Tie the cord into a double knot, gathering up the stapled end of the fan. Make sure the fan is securely in place.

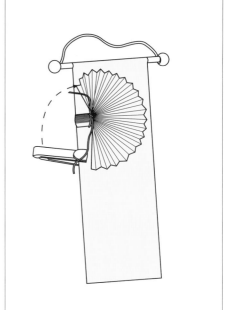

19 Spread out the fan and staple each side to the Washi strip. Arrange the folds in the fan so that they are evenly distributed. Hot glue under the fan to keep it in place.

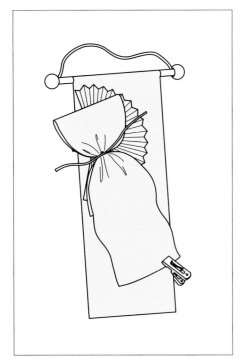

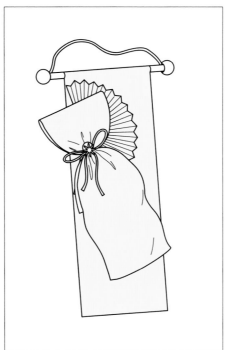

20 Place the half bow on top of the fan and tie securely in place. Place the bottom portion of the bow (step 6) on the opposite corner, puff it up, and glue in place. Secure with a clothes pin until dry.

21 Tie in some flowers and leaves with the cord, using either bows or knots.

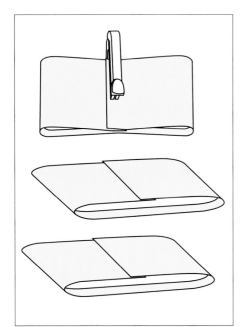

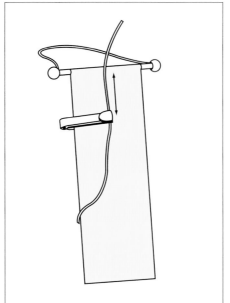

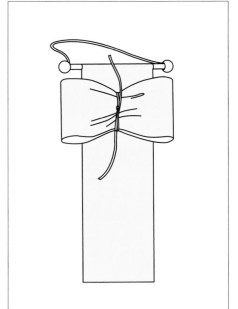

22 To make the bows, take the two narrow strips of Washi prepared in step 8. Fold the ends towards the center, placing one end over the other, and staple together.

23 To assemble the bow-style obi, fold the 10" (HS/FS – 25") length of cord in half and place it 1" (HS –4"; FS – 5 1/2") below the center of the dowel. Staple the cord to the Washi strip.

24 Place one of the double-folded bows horizontally in the center of the vertical cord. Tie the cord, gathering up the center of the bow. Make sure the bow is securely in place.

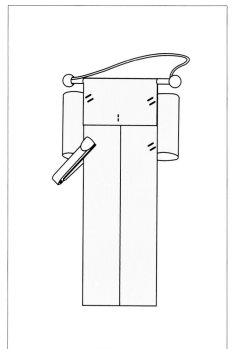

25 Turn the obi over and carefully staple each end of the bow to the Washi.

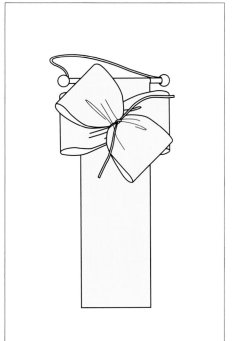

26 Place the second bow on top of the first one and tie securely with the cord. Shape the bow and arrange it so that it is slightly slanted.

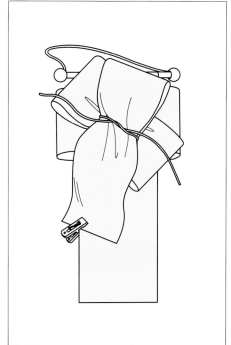

27 Place the half bow on top of the second bow and tie securely in place. Place the bottom portion of the bow on the opposite corner, puff it up, and glue in place. Secure with a clothes pin until dry.

28 Complete the obi by tying in some flowers and leaves with the cord, using either a bow or a knot.

Covered Eggs

Throughtout history, the egg has been a powerful symbol of hope and new life in many different cultures. The purity and strength of the egg's elongated, symmetrical form have made it a classic shape and motif for design. Blown hen, duck, goose, quail – even ostrich – eggs can all be decorated with Washi to produce stunning and original objets d'art, whether for enhancing an Easter table, for seasonal decorations, or for permanent display in bowls and baskets. Although the blown eggs are delicate, they become highly durable when covered with Washi and brushed several times with shellac. Washi covered eggs are especially elegant when covered with gold and black paper; festive when covered with bright colored paper; warm and inspiring when covered with the colors of Fall. The creative possibilities of embellishing eggs of different sizes with Washi makes this one of the most popular of all Washi projects.

SECTIONS IN THIS CHAPTER
- Preparing the Eggs
- Basic Washi Covered Eggs
- Covering Quail Eggs
- Collage Covered Eggs
- Washi Egg Tree Ornaments
- Shellacking Washi Covered Eggs

Preparing the Eggs

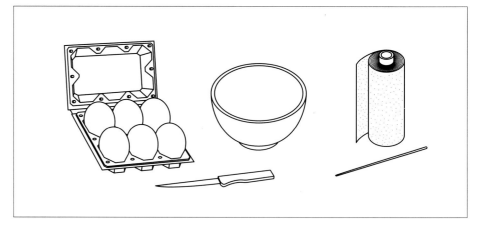

EQUIPMENT AND MATERIALS

- 6 hen's eggs at room temperature in a cardboard carton
- Small pointed knife
- Paper towels
- Long toothpick or wooden skewer
- Microwave safe dish or plate

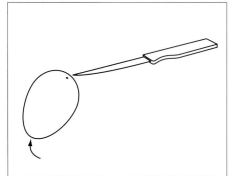

1 Take one egg and carefully make a 1/8–1/4" hole at each end with the small pointed knife.

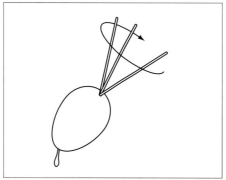

2 Insert the toothpick or skewer into one of the holes and jiggle it around until the egg yolk is broken.

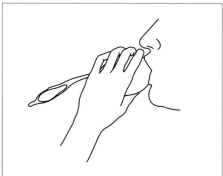

3 Blow into one hole until all the egg mixture comes out the other end. Run some water into the egg, shake it, and blow again. Repeat until the water is clear. Repeat the process with the remaining eggs.

4 If you have a microwave oven, cover a microwave safe dish with paper towels and place the eggs on the towels with one hole facing down. Microwave for 20 seconds on High. Change the paper towels and repeat. Put the eggs back into the carton and leave to dry for a few hours.

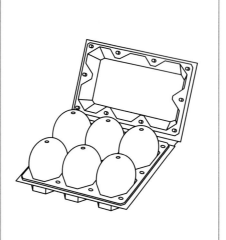

5 If you do not have a microwave oven, put the eggs back into the cardboard carton and wait at least a day or overnight for the eggs to dry. If water from the eggs continues to wet the carton, this indicates that the eggs are still too wet to be covered with Washi.

TIP
The eggs must be completely dry before they are covered. If water leaks out of them, causing the Washi to become too wet, peel off the Washi and let the eggs dry out completely before recovering them.

Basic Washi Covered Eggs

EQUIPMENT AND MATERIALS

- 6 blown hen's eggs
- 1/4 sheet of printed Washi
- Small paint brush
- White craft paste or glue
- Small cup or bowl
- Measuring tape
- Tracing paper and pencil
- Small sharp scissors
- Damp kitchen towel or washcloth
- Wooden dowel (12" x 1/8")

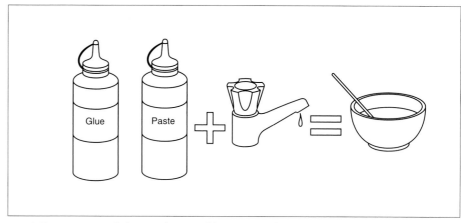

6 Mix 1/4 cup of glue and 1–2 tablespoons of tap water. The glue should be easy to spread but not too watery.

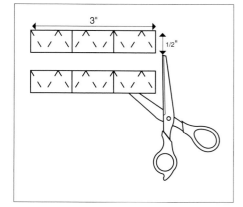

7 To reinforce the holes at each end of the egg, cut two 3" x 1/2" strips out of scraps of Washi. Cut the strips up into triangles. The borders of Washi can be used.

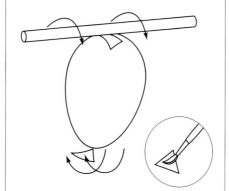

8 Glue one or two triangles, plain side up, over each hole. Cover any cracks in the eggs in the same way. Use the wooden dowel to smooth out any lumps or wrinkles.

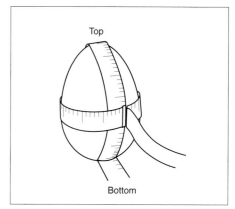

9 Measure all the eggs. One of the pattern sizes should fit the eggs, which may vary a little in size.

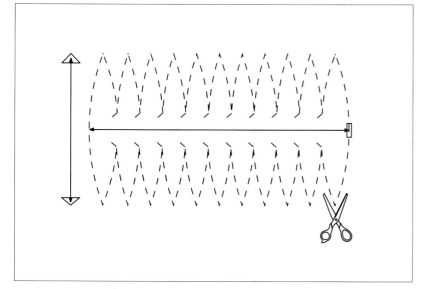

10 Measure the egg pattern on page 62 to see which size best fits the eggs. Trace the pattern using the tracing paper, and increase or decrease the size as needed.

HEN'S EGG PATTERN

Trace the required pattern. Lay it on the Washi and cut out the pattern and Washi together. With practice you will be able to cut the pattern and several layers of Washi at the same time.

Small

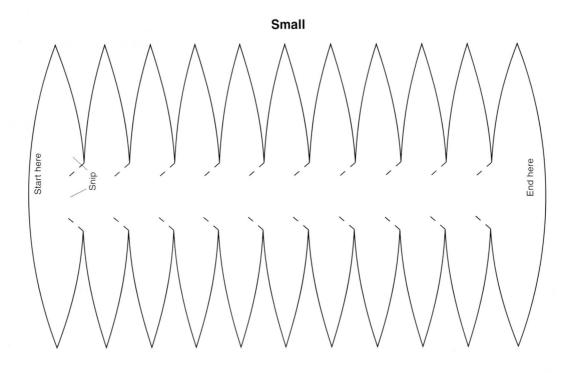

Large

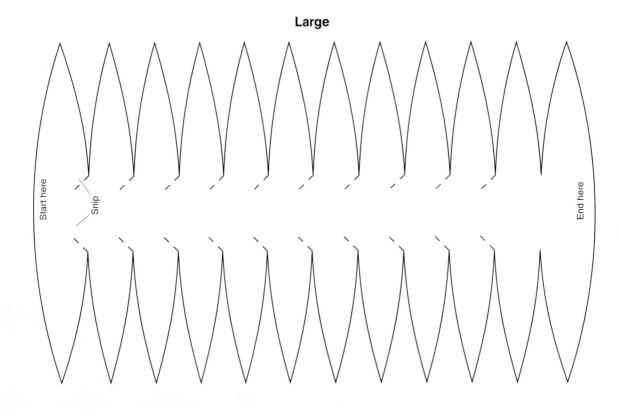

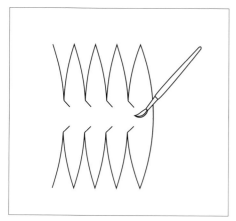

11 Brush glue on the first strip of Washi, starting at the end indicated on the pattern.

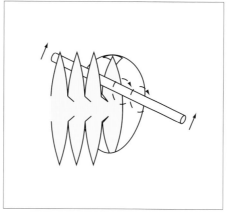

12 Center the strip, making sure that both ends reach the top (north) and bottom (south) of the egg. Roll out any lumps and creases with the wooden dowel.

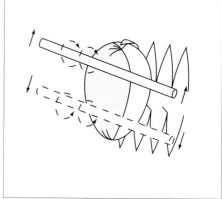

13 Continue adding strips, one at a time, around the egg making sure each piece reaches the top and bottom.

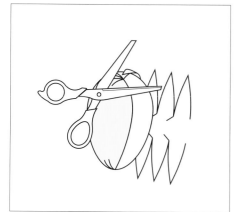

14 Halfway around the egg, start trimming the top and bottom ends of the Washi so that the points meet nicely and are centered at both ends of the egg.

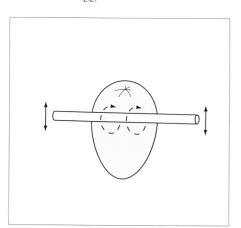

15 Use the dowel to smooth the Washi. Complete all six eggs and let them dry for 2–4 hours before shellacking them.

TIPS
- Always put the glue on the Washi, not the egg, and always glue one strip at a time.
- Use a damp cloth frequently to wipe any drips of glue, and to keep your hands clean.
- Do not apply too much pressure when using the dowel to smooth the Washi or the eggs will break.

Covering Quail Eggs

Quail eggs make wonderful tree ornaments, especially at festival times, such as Christmas or Easter! They also look charming arranged on a table in little baskets or in a nest made of twigs or shredded paper. The Washi selected for covering the eggs can match the color palette of the festival or season, or a room.

EQUIPMENT AND MATERIALS

- 6 blown quail eggs (follow steps 1–5)
- 1/8 sheet of printed Washi
- Small paint brush
- White craft paste or glue
- Small cup or bowl
- Measuring tape
- Tracing paper and pencil
- Small sharp scissors
- Damp kitchen towel or washcloth
- Wooden dowel (12" x 1/8")

16 Follow steps 7–9 on page 61. Position the Washi strips carefully as quail eggs are larger at the top and narrower at the bottom, the reverse of hen's eggs.

NOTE
Quail eggs are very fragile. It is important to take extra care when blowing the egg yolk out so that the eggs do not break. If possible, use a one-hole egg blower that can be purchased at most craft stores, and blow the egg out at the larger end, not the pointed end.

QUAIL'S EGG PATTERN

Trace the required pattern. Lay it on the Washi and cut out the pattern and Washi together. With practice you will be able to cut the pattern and several layers of Washi at the same time.

Small

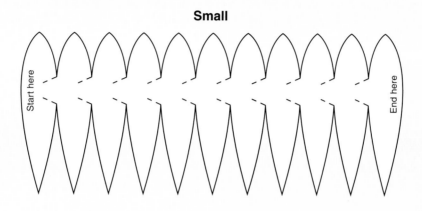

Medium

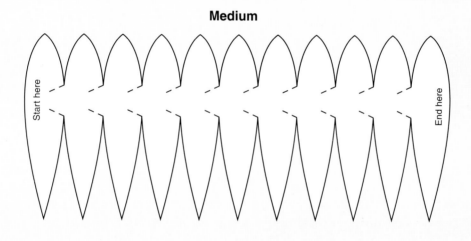

Large

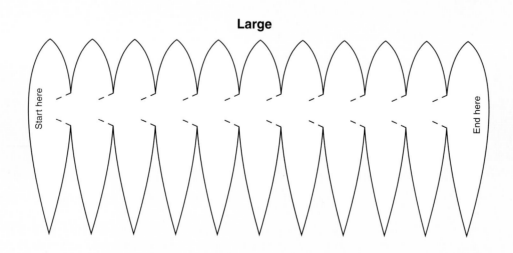

Collage Covered Eggs

This is a great way to use up scraps of Washi left over from other projects! As it is the simplest method of covering eggs with Washi, it is also an ideal way to start children off on Washi covered eggs. Different effects can be achieved by choosing a single color scheme or by combining complementary or clashing colors.

EQUIPMENT AND MATERIALS

- 6 blown hen's eggs (follow steps 1–5)
- 1/4 sheet of printed Washi or scraps of Washi
- Small paint brush
- White craft paste or glue
- Small cup or bowl
- Small sharp scissors
- Damp kitchen towel or washcloth
- Dowel (12" x 1/8)
- Tablecloth to protect working surface

17 Follow steps 7–9 on page 61.

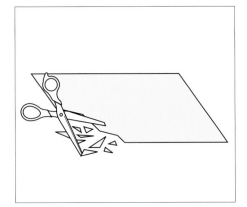

18 Cut the Washi into triangles as in step 7, or into small triangles of different sizes.

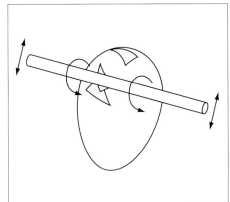

19 Glue the triangles, one by one, on each egg until it is completely covered. Roll out any lumps and creases with the dowel as you work.

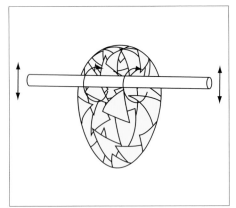

20 Use the dowel to smooth the Washi triangles. Complete all six eggs and let them dry for 2–4 hours before shellacking them.

Washi Hanging Egg Ornaments

Washi egg ornaments are great for decorating a holiday tree. They also look stunning when suspended from decorative ornament hangers.

EQUIPMENT AND MATERIALS

- 6 Washi covered eggs
- 6 bead caps (18 mm) in gold or silver
- 1 yard of thin gold or silver cord cut into 6" lengths
- Small sharp scissors
- Small hot glue gun and glue sticks
- Cardboard egg carton
- Large piece of cardboard to protect working surface

21 Fold each 6" length of cord in half and tie the ends in a knot. Pull the folded end through the hole in the bead cap, leaving the knot inside. Tie another knot if the hole is too large. Cut off the excess cord.

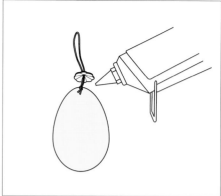

22 Put hot glue on the knotted end of the cord and quickly glue it to the narrow top of the egg.

23 Do the same with the other five eggs.

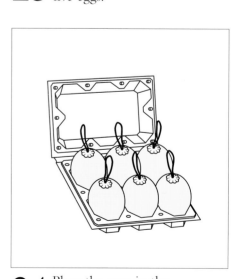

24 Place the eggs in the cardboard egg carton and leave them to dry for at least 1–2 hours before covering with shellac.

Shellacking Washi Covered Eggs

EQUIPMENT AND MATERIALS

- 6 Washi covered eggs
- Plastic multi-armed coat hanger
- Large cookie sheet to catch shellac drips
- Small hot glue gun and glue sticks
- Paint brush
- 6 long straight pins (1/2") with large heads
- 8 oz bottle or can of water-based shellac
- Covered container for storing the shellac
- Small deep bowl for dipping the eggs
- Cardboard egg carton
- Cutting blade
- Cream or white cotton doily (12")
- Tablecloth to protect working surface

TIPS

- Make sure that your Washi covered eggs are completely dry before you begin, otherwise the Washi will peel off when the eggs are dipped into the shellac.
- Only use water-based shellac. Oil- or gas-based shellac will eat away at the Washi as it is a natural fiber.
- Pour the shellac that has dripped on to the cookie sheet back into the covered storage container so that it can be reused.
- Wash the cookie sheet immediately as it will be very hard to clean after the shellac dries!
- An aluminum foil cookie sheet or a pizza pan can be used instead of a cookie sheet and then disposed of.
- Repeat the shellacking process 4–6 times to get a good shine and to strengthen the eggs.
- Let the shellacked eggs dry for one or two days before placing them in a bowl or basket, to prevent them from sticking together.

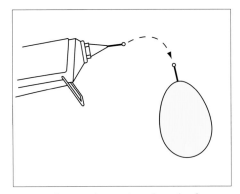

25 Insert the pointed end of a pin 1/2" into the barrel of the hot glue gun. Then carefully stick the end of the pin into the hole at the top of the egg.

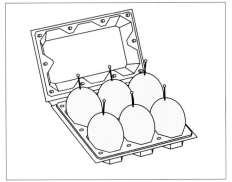

26 When all six eggs are done, put them in the egg carton and let them dry for 1–2 hours before shellacking them.

27 Holding the pinhead, carefully dip each egg into the bowl of shellac. Push the eggs down as they will float.

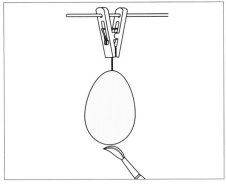

28 Clip the pinhead to the plastic coat hanger. Place the cookie sheet below to catch the drips. Complete all six eggs, then dab away any excess drips 2–3 times. Leave the eggs to dry for at least an hour before redipping them.

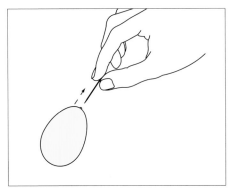

29 Remove the dried eggs from the hanger. Then use the cutting blade to carefully trim around the area where the glue and pin meet. When loosened, pull out the pin.

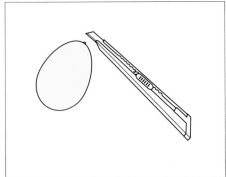

30 Trim off any excess dried hot glue.

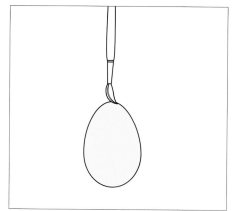

31 If necessary, brush some shellac on the top of the egg where the pin was.

32 To shellac Washi egg ornaments, hold the cord above the bead cap to dip the eggs into the shellac. Then follow step 28.

33 If you do not have a multi-armed coat hanger, hold each egg in turn and carefully brush a little shellac on one side. Place on the cotton doily, wet side up. When completely dry, shellac the other side of the eggs. Repeat 3–4 times.

Egg Bowl or Basket

Although Washi covered eggs may be displayed in a nest made of twigs, straw, grasses or shredded packing paper, or in a store-bought basket or bowl, the beauty and colors of the eggs – and the talents of the crafter! – will be highlighted if the eggs are displayed in a Washi covered bowl or basket specially made from milk cartons. A bowl or basket of eggs can add the finishing touch to a room, serve as a quick and easy table decoration at a dinner party, or make the perfect gift.

EQUIPMENT AND MATERIALS FOR ONE BOWL OR BASKET

- 1 square of printed Washi (101/2" x 101/2")
- 1 square of solid or printed Washi (9" x 9")
- 1 strip of printed Washi (14" x 11/2") for basket handle
- 4 milk cartons (quart size), washed and dried
- 3 squares of thick construction paper (31/2" x 31/2") for petal templates
- 1 square of thick construction paper (21/2" x 21/2") for base-fill template
- 2 squares of thick construction paper (3" x 3") for inside and outside base
- 1 strip of thick construction paper (5/8" x 14") for the basket handle
- Roll of transparent tape (Scotch tape)
- Tracing paper and pencil
- Small sharp scissors
- Cutting blade
- Ruler or measuring tape
- Glue stick
- Small stapler
- Damp washcloth
- Ribbons/Flowers (optional)

PREPARING THE CARTONS

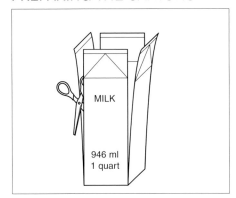

1 Follow these steps for all four cartons. First, cut down all four sides of the milk carton with the scissors.

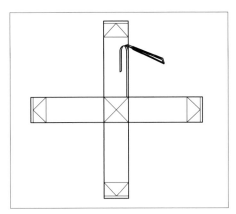

2 Open up the milk carton and lay it flat on the table, wrong side up. With the cutting blade, remove the seam that holds the carton together.

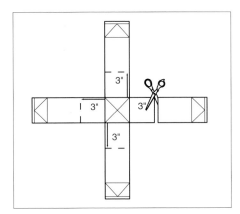

3 Measure 3" up each side of the carton from the base crease and draw a line across. Cut off the top sections and put aside for later use.

PETAL TEMPLATE A

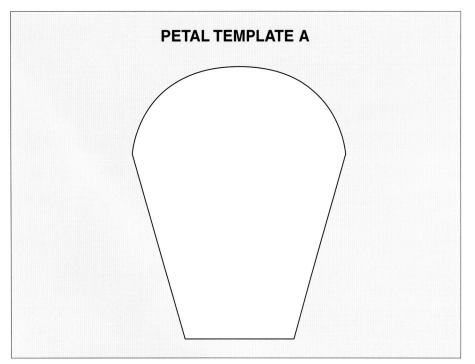

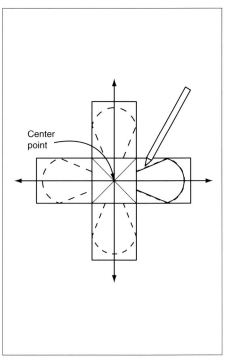

Center point

4 Using tracing paper, trace petal template A. Cut out the template from the 3½" x 3½" square of thick construction paper.

5 Draw lines down the middle of the carton sections, then find the center point on the bottom square. Place the template on the crease line of all four sections and draw around it.

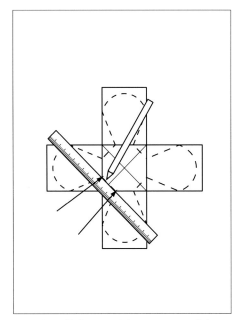

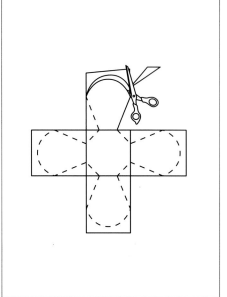

BASE-FILL TEMPLATE

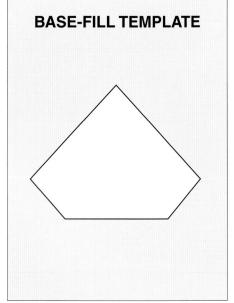

6 On all four inside corners of the milk carton, draw a connecting line from one corner (A) to the other (B).

7 Carefully cut around and in between each petal section, making sure not to cut the parts that join the petals to the base!

8 Using tracing paper, trace the base-fill template. Cut out the template from the 2½" x 2½" square of thick construction paper.

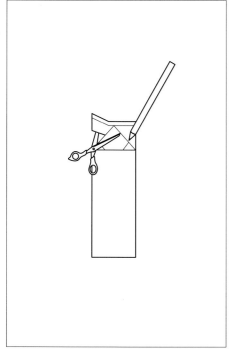

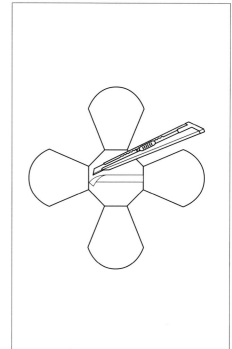

9 Draw around the base-fill template on the pouring spout of the milk carton, then cut it out. Repeat so that there are two base-fill pieces for each carton.

10 Using the glue stick, glue the base-fill pieces to the bottom of the carton to make it level. Trim the pieces so that they fit nicely on the bottom. Tape down, if necessary.

11 Turn the carton over, right side up. With the blade, cut off the top seam that runs across the middle of the carton. This will level out the base. Turn the carton over and check that it lies flat. If not, keep trimming.

ASSEMBLING THE BOWL/BASKET

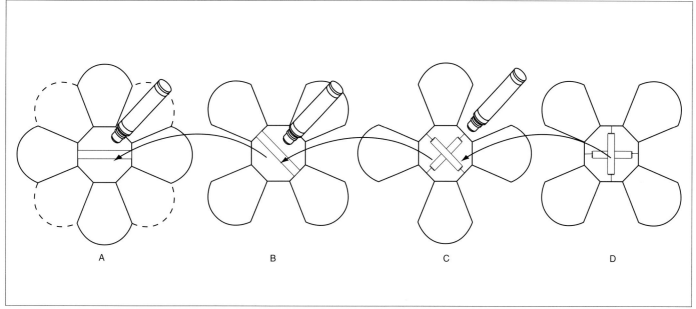

A   B   C   D

12 Place the first carton on the table with the outside facing upward (A). Spread some glue on the base of the first carton, then place the second carton, with the outside facing up, on top of it (B). The petals should fall in between those of the first carton, not directly on top of them. Next, spread glue on the base of the second carton, then place the third carton, wrong side up, on top of it (C). The petals should fall in between those of the second carton, matching up with those of the first carton. Now, spread glue on the base of the third carton and place the fourth carton, wrong side up, on top of it (D). The petals should fall in between those of the third carton, matching up with those of the second carton.

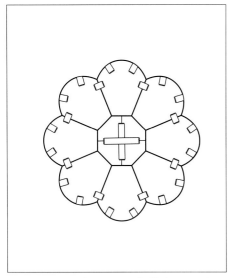

PETAL TEMPLATE B

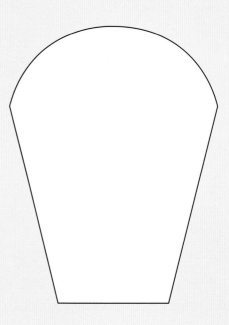

13 Tape the tops of all the petal sections together and then the sides, both on the inside and outside of the bowl/basket. If the outer petals are a little shorter than the inside ones, even all petals out as best you can and then tape them together.

14 Using tracing paper, trace petal templates B and C. Cut out the templates from the 31/2" x 31/2" squares of thick construction paper.

PETAL TEMPLATE C

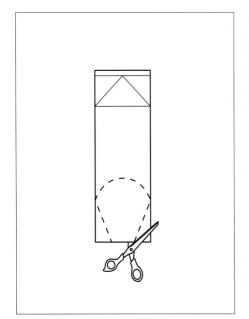

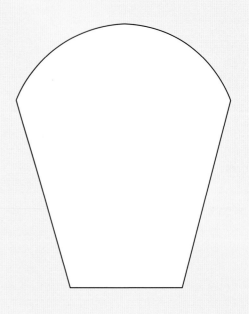

15 Draw around the templates on the excess milk carton sections that you put aside in step 3. Cut out four pieces of each template.

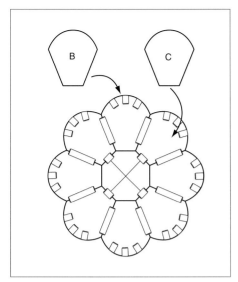

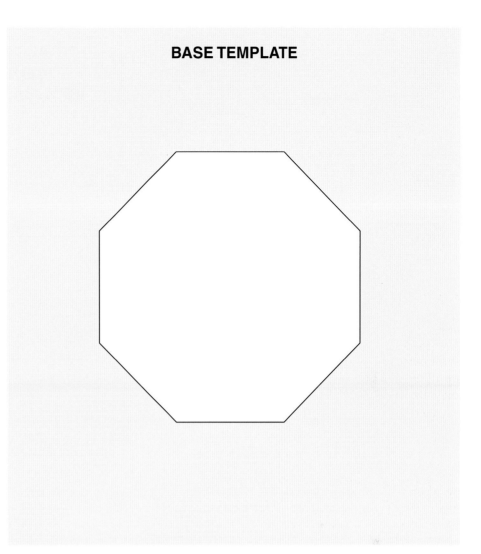

BASE TEMPLATE

16 Use the eight petal pieces to level out the inside and outside of the bowl/basket where the petal sections are not joined to the central base. Position the four petals cut from template B on the outside of the bowl/basket and tape in place. Repeat with the petals cut from template C on the inside of the bowl/basket.

17 Trace and cut out the base template, then cut out two bases from the 3" x 3" squares of thick construction paper.

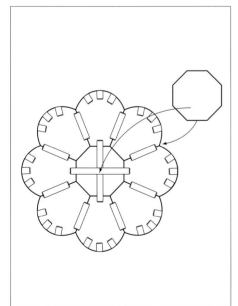

18 Glue and tape the base pieces to the center bottom inside and outside of the bowl/basket.

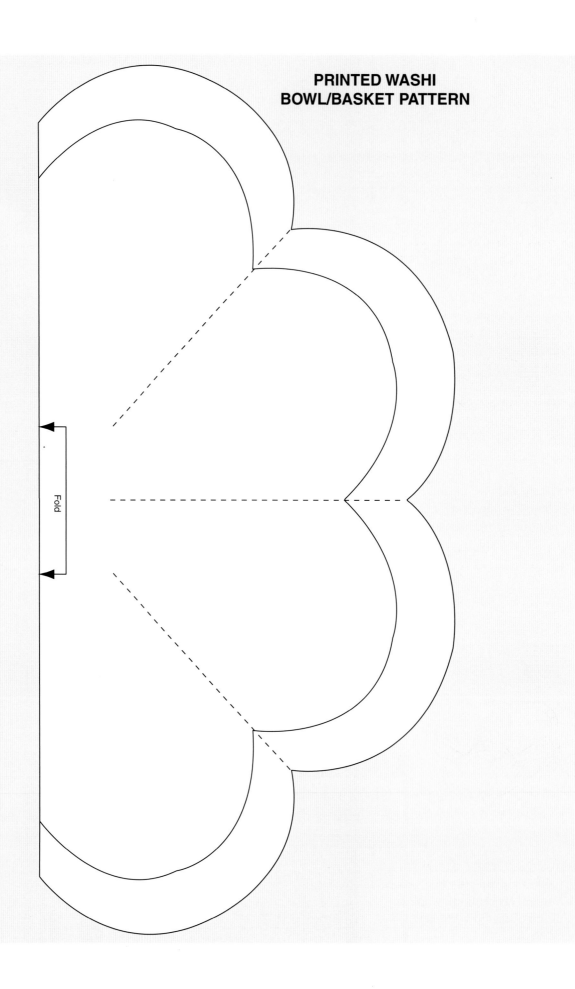

**PRINTED WASHI
BOWL/BASKET PATTERN**

Fold

COVERING THE BOWL/BASKET

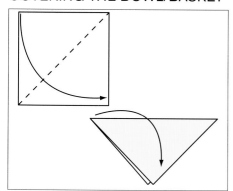

19 Take the 10½" x 10½" square of printed Washi and fold it in half to form a triangle.

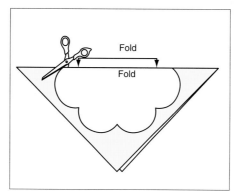

20 Trace and cut out the printed Washi bowl/basket pattern on page 76. Place it on the fold side of the printed Washi triangle and cut around it.

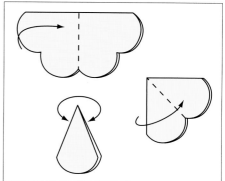

21 Fold the printed Washi in half, then in quarters, and then in eighths. Crease all the edges.

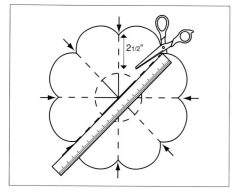

22 Open the printed Washi and lay it on the table, wrong side up. Measure 2½" down the crease on all eight sides, then cut down each side towards the center.

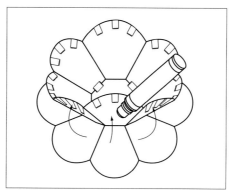

23 Spread glue on the milk carton base and place it in the middle of the printed Washi. Turn the bowl/basket over and smooth out the Washi. Put glue on each petal section and pull up the printed Washi.

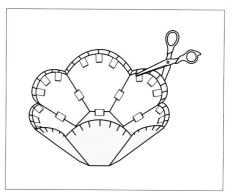

24 Make sure the Washi is smooth and the petal sections are nicely overlapping. Then snip the printed Washi, at ¼" intervals, all around the top petals.

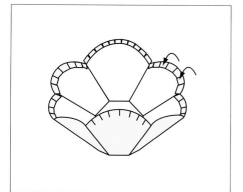

25 If you are making the Washi egg bowl, glue down all the snipped Washi sections. If you are making the Washi egg basket, glue down all but two petals, on opposite sides.

26 To make the handle for the basket, spread glue on the wrong side of the 14" x 1 1/2" strip of printed Washi and roll on to the 14" x 5/8" strip of thick construction paper. Smooth out.

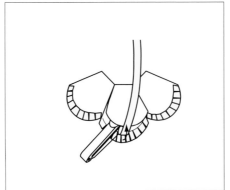

27 Insert the ends of the handle about 1" between the layers of the two petals that are towards the inside of the bowl. Staple together about three times to secure in place.

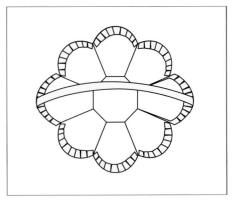

28 Carefully glue the snipped Washi down over the petals. Trim the snipped Washi and tuck it in the area between the petals and the handle.

FINISHING THE BOWL/BASKET

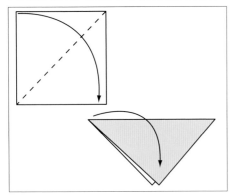

29 Take the 9" x 9" square of solid Washi (you can also use printed washi if you prefer) and fold it in half to form a triangle.

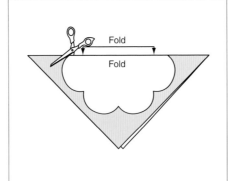

30 Trace and cut out the solid Washi bowl/basket pattern on page 79. Place it on the fold side of the solid Washi triangle and cut around it.

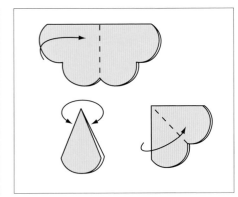

31 Fold the solid Washi in half, then in quarters, and then in eighths. Crease all the edges.

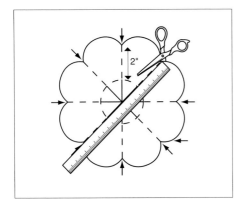

32 Open the solid or printed Washi and lay it on the table, wrong side up. Measure 2" down the crease on all eight sides, then cut down each towards the center.

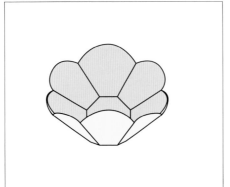

33 Spread glue on the inside base and on each inside petal of the completed bowl/basket. Carefully smooth on the solid or printed Washi, matching up the petals.

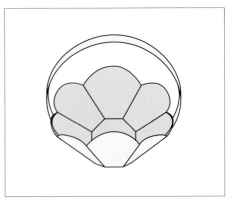

34 Trim off any excess solid or printed Washi at the top of the petals. Leave the bowl/basket to dry thoroughly before shellacking it and filling with Washi covered eggs.

PRINTED OR SOLID WASHI BOWL/BASKET PATTERN

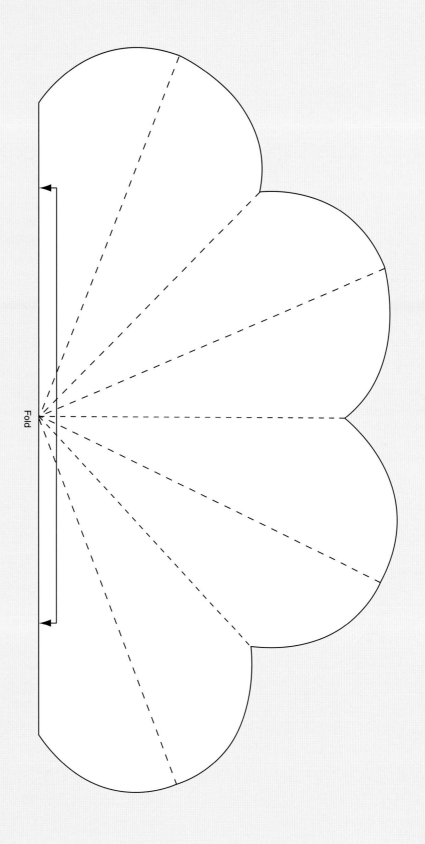

Fold

Table Toppers

Table Toppers are a novel and personal way of decorating tables for special occasions. Surprise the guests at a birthday, wedding or farewell with table toppers showing photographs of the life of the guest(s) of honor or other accessories suited to the occasion and the people present. The shape of a table topper can be changed by using a shorter or longer tube and a round instead of a square base.

EQUIPMENT AND MATERIALS FOR MAKING ONE TABLE TOPPER

- 1 photograph (81/2" x 6")
- 1 empty paper towel roll
- 2 empty toilet paper rolls
- 2 squares of cardboard
  (31/2" x 31/2" x 1/8")
- 1 rectangle of printed Washi (6" x 2")
- 1 square of printed Washi (51/2" x 51/2")
- 1 square of printed Washi (41/2" x 41/2")
- 1 square of solid Washi (3" x 3")
- 1 square of printed Washi (6" x 6") for the crane
- 2 pieces of coordinating ribbon (11" x 1/4")
- Small artificial flowers for decoration
- Tape
- Small sharp scissors
- Cutting blade
- Hot glue gun and glue sticks
- Glue stick
- Pencil and ruler
- Tracing paper

NOTE
The sizes of paper towel and toilet paper tubes may differ according to brand. Sometimes toilet paper rolls will fit inside paper towel tubes, sometimes on the outside. Adapt the instructions accordingly.

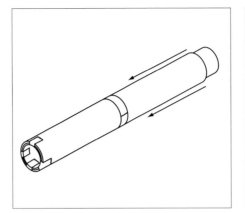

1 Insert the paper towel tube into the two toilet paper tubes. Slide it all the way down the paper towel tube and tape the ends where the tubes meet. Then tape the seam that joins the two toilet paper tubes.

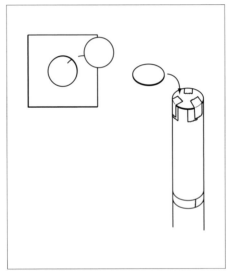

3 Cut out the traced circle with the cutting blade and secure it with tape.

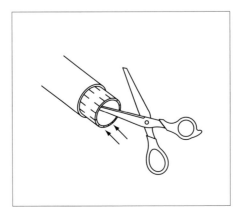

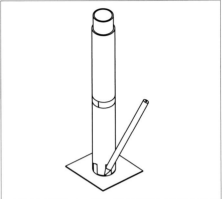

2 Place the taped end of the tube in the center of one of the cardboard squares and draw around the base.

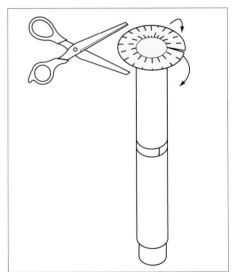

4 Trace the pattern below, then cut out the circle from the 41/2" square of printed Washi. Spread glue on the wrong side of the circle and place it on top of the covered end of the tube. Snip around the edges of the Washi and smooth the edges down the side of the tube.

5 At the other end, use the scissors to snip the protruding paper towel tube at 1/4" intervals to where it meets the toilet paper tube.

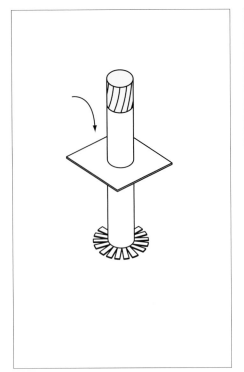

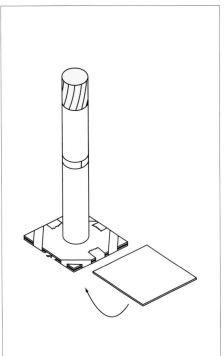

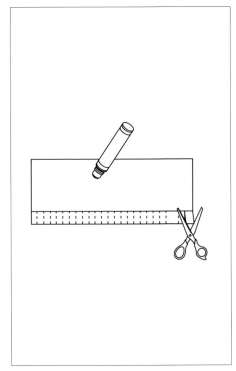

6 Spread out the 1/4" sections. Place the cut out cardboard square over the Washi covered tube and push it down to the spread out bottom.

7 Place the second square of cardboard underneath the bottom of the first piece and tape all the sides together. Snip off any excess tube protruding out the sides.

8 Take the 6" x 2" rectangle of printed Washi and fold over 1/2" on one side. Make 1/2" cuts every 1/4" along the folded end. Spread glue on the wrong side of the Washi.

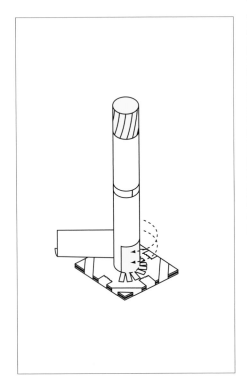

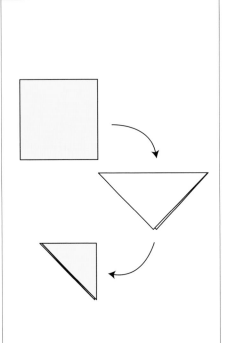

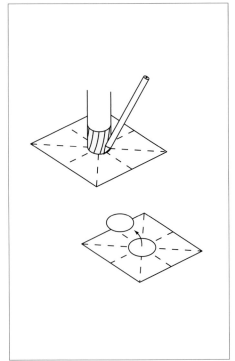

9 Paste the printed Washi around the bottom of the tube, spreading the 1/4" sections out around the cardboard base.

10 Take the 51/2" x 51/2" square of printed Washi. Fold it in half, then in half again. Crease all the sides.

11 Open up the creased Washi square. Place the top end of the paper towel tube in the center of the Washi, trace around it, then cut it out.

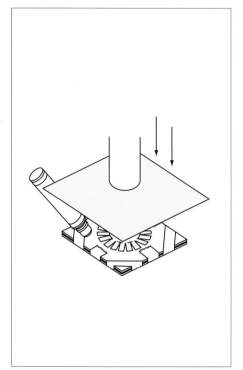

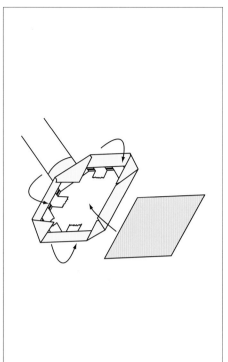

12 Spread glue on the cardboard square. Place the square of printed Washi over the top of the tube, push it to the bottom and smooth out.

13 Turn the tube over. Tidy the base by gluing and folding over the sides of the Washi. Then glue the square of solid Washi to the base.

CIRCLE PATTERN

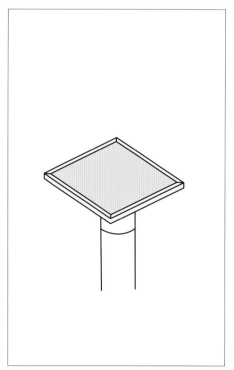

14 Turn the tube upside down and put it aside until the base is completely dry.

PREPARING THE PHOTOGRAPH

15 Choose a standard portrait photo (10" x 8") and cut it down to 8 1/2" x 6". Make sure the subject can be clearly seen.

16 Alternatively, scan the photo you have selected to fit the exact measurement (8 1/2" x 6") and print it out.

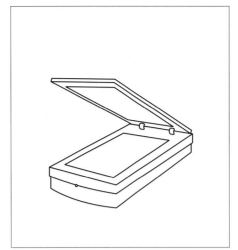

17 Place the photo around the tube. Position the main subject so that it faces one of the corners of the base.

FINISHING THE TABLE TOPPER

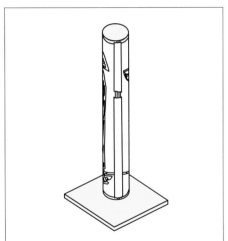

18 Carefully tape the edges of the photo together where they meet at the center back of the tube.

19 Tie the two 11" ribbons into bows. Glue one bow on the corner of the base where the main subject is facing. Glue some flowers around the base and near the bow.

20 Use the 6" x 6" square of printed Washi to make an origami crane (see pages 48–9). Glue more flowers, the second bow and the origami crane on top of the tube.

Refrigerator Magnets

These refrigerator magnets, which exemplify the elegance of the traditional Japanese dress, are simple to make and yet creative. The colors of the magnets can be coordinated to match your kitchen or office. Extra flowers and ribbons can be added to the girl's hair. Magnets make great little hostess gifts or small crafts to sell at bazaars.

EQUIPMENT AND MATERIALS FOR ONE BOY MAGNET AND ONE GIRL MAGNET

- 1 rectangle of printed Washi (6" x 3") for the boy's happy coat
- 1 rectangle of printed Washi (6" x 3") for the girl's kimono
- 1 rectangle of printed Washi (6" x 2 1/2") for the girl's kimono sleeves
- 2 strips of printed Washi (3" x 1/2") for the obi (select contrasting patterns or colors)
- 2 strips of solid Washi (6" x 1/2") for the neck trims
- 2 white poster board rectangles (2 1/2" x 1 1/2") for the bodies
- 4 poster board circles (1 1/2") for the heads
- 2 solid black crimped Washi rectangles (6 1/2" x 2") for the hair
- 1 cord (7" x 1/8") for the boy's happy coat
- 1 coordinating strip of solid Washi (1" x 1/4") for the girl's hair bow
- 4 magnet squares or circles (1/2")
- Fine red and black felt tip markers
- Small sharp scissors
- Glue stick
- Tracing paper and pencil
- Ruler

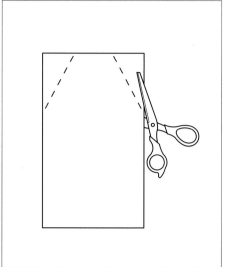

1 Trace the body pattern, then cut out two bodies from the poster board, one for the boy magnet and one for the girl magnet.

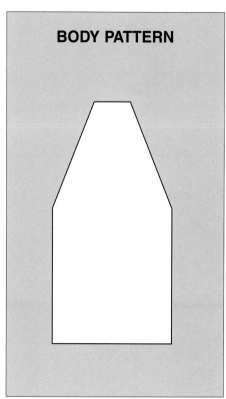

BODY PATTERN

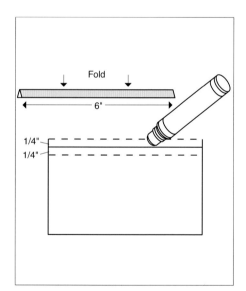

2 Take one of the printed Washi rectangles (6" x 3") and one strip of solid Washi (6" x 1/2"). Fold the strip in half lengthwise and spread glue on one side. Place the glued side at the top of the plain (back) side of the Washi. The other half of the strip will fold over to the front of the printed Washi. Repeat with the second Washi rectangle and strip.

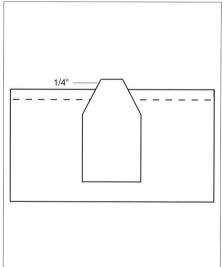

3 With the plain side of the Washi facing upward, place the poster board body in the middle with the neck extending 1/4" above the solid Washi strip. Glue down. Repeat with the second Washi rectangle and poster board.

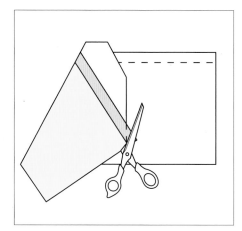

4 Fold the right-hand side of the happy coat/kimono over the body. The happy coat/kimono should fall naturally against the neck. Snip excess washi off at the side.

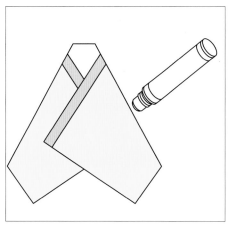

5 Fold the left-hand side of the happy coat/kimono over the right-hand side and paste down.

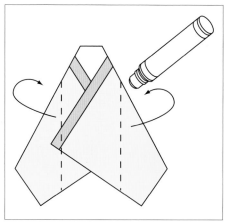

6 Fold both sides of the happy coat/kimono against the straight sides of the body board and take the ends to the back. Paste down.

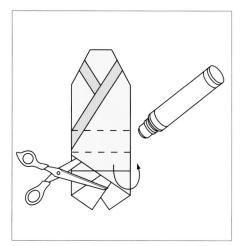

7 Trim off any excess Washi at the bottom, then fold 1" of Washi towards the back of the body and paste down.

8 Take the long narrow strip of printed Washi (3" x 1/2") and paste it around the waist of the happy coat/kimono to form the obi.

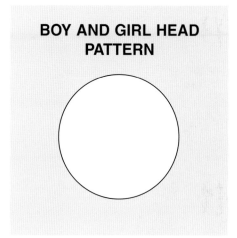

BOY AND GIRL HEAD PATTERN

9 Trace and cut out the head pattern from poster board. Cut two pieces.

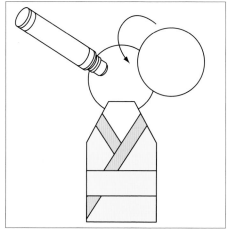

10 Paste the poster board circles on both sides of the neck.

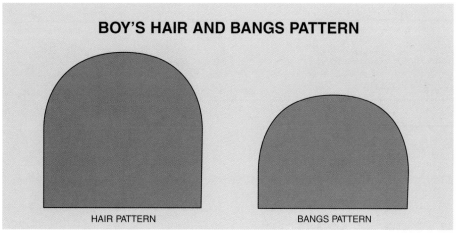

BOY'S HAIR AND BANGS PATTERN

HAIR PATTERN

BANGS PATTERN

11 Trace the patterns for the hair and bangs.

FINISHING THE BOY MAGNET

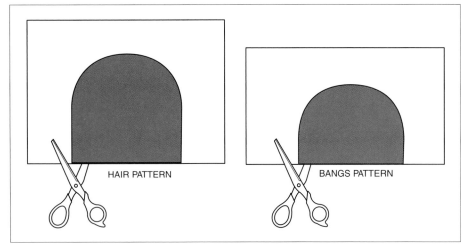

12 Cut the bangs and hair out of the rectangle of crimped solid Washi (6" x 2½"). Make sure that the grain of the crimps is vertical.

13 Paste the bangs to the front of the head.

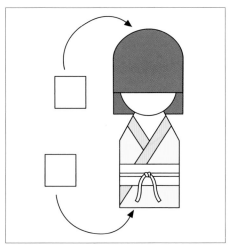

14 Paste the hair to the back of the head, making sure the top of the hair is lined up with the top of the bangs.

15 Tie the obi cord (7" x 1/8") around the waist, centering it in the middle of the obi. Tie a double knot in the center front.

16 Paste the magnets on the back of the boy's body. Trim off any excess obi cord.

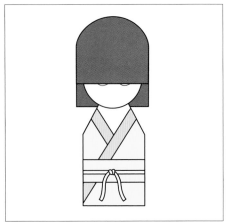

17 Using the fine black and red felt tip markers, draw the eyes and mouth on the face.

GIRL'S HAIR AND BANGS PATTERN

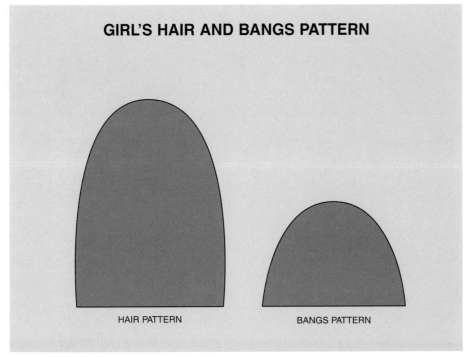

HAIR PATTERN

BANGS PATTERN

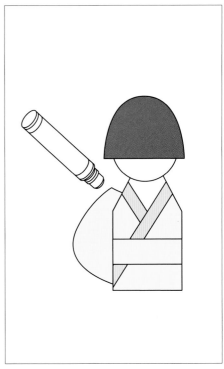

18 Trace the patterns for the girl's hair and bangs, and then cut the bangs and hair out of the rectangle of crimped solid Washi (6" x 2 1/2").

19 Paste the bangs to the front of the head.

KIMONO PATTERN

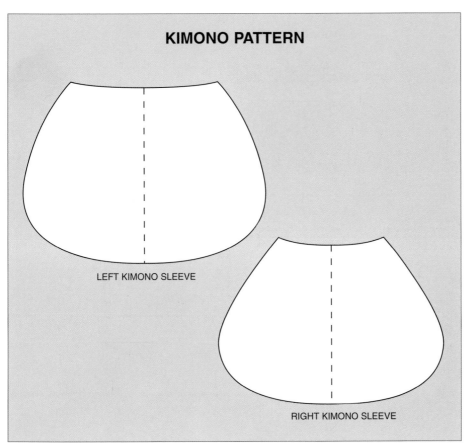

LEFT KIMONO SLEEVE

RIGHT KIMONO SLEEVE

20 Trace and cut out the sleeves for the kimono.

21 Fold the left kimono sleeve in half and paste together. Then paste the sleeve to the left-hand back of the body.

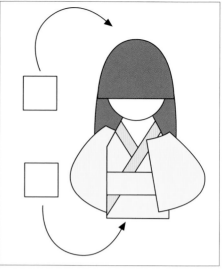

22 Paste the hair to the back of the head, making sure the top of the hair is lined up with the top of the bangs.

23 Fold the right kimono sleeve in half and paste together. Then paste it to the front right-hand side of the body.

24 Paste the magnets on the back of the girl's body.

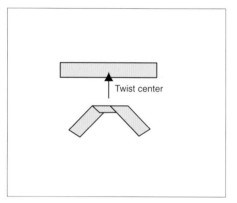

Twist center

25 Take the narrow strip of coordinating solid Washi (1" x 1/4") and twist it a couple of times in the center to form a bow.

26 Using the fine black and red felt tip markers, draw the eyes and mouth on the face. Finish off by placing the bow on the girl's hair.